# THE HOUSE OF HARDSHIPS & DECEITS

**SELEBOGO STEVENS HLONGWANE**

*Tie Publisher*

First published by Tie Publishers 2024

Copyright © 2024 by Selebogo Stevens Hlongwane

All rights reserved. No part of this publication may be reproduced, stored or transmitted in any form or by any means, electronic, mechanical, photocopying, recording, scanning, or otherwise without written permission from the publisher. It is illegal to copy this book, post it to a website, or distribute it by any other means without permission.

This novel is entirely a work of fiction. The names, characters and incidents portrayed in it are the work of the author's imagination. Any resemblance to actual persons, living or dead, events or localities is entirely coincidental.

Selebogo Stevens Hlongwane asserts the moral right to be identified as the author of this work.

Selebogo Stevens Hlongwane has no responsibility for the persistence or accuracy of URLs for external or third-party Internet Websites referred to in this publication and does not guarantee that any content on such Websites is, or will remain, accurate or appropriate.

Designations used by companies to distinguish their products are often claimed as trademarks. All brand names and product names used in this book and on its cover are trade names, service marks, trademarks and registered trademarks of their respective owners. The publishers and the book are not associated with any product or vendor mentioned in this book. None of the companies referenced within the book have endorsed the book.

First edition

ISBN: 978-0-7961-4666-3

This book was professionally typeset by

Tie Publishers

To the resilient spirits of Mamelodi Township, whose lives are etched into the very fabric of this narrative. This book is dedicated to the men and women, the families and communities, who forged their destinies amidst the challenges of displacement, racial divides, and economic hardships.

In honor of those who, against the backdrop of adversity, found strength in community, solace in culture, and hope in education. Your stories, struggles, and triumphs have woven the vibrant tapestry of Mamelodi, and through these pages, we celebrate your unwavering courage and the indomitable spirit that defines this extraordinary township.

May this dedication stand as a testament to the generations who have shaped Mamelodi's history, and to those who continue to contribute to its vibrant legacy. In the words of your resilience, in the echoes of your melodies, this book is dedicated to you— the heartbeat of Mamelodi.

*In the heart of Mamelodi Township, where melodies echo through the struggles of relocation and resistance, this book unfolds the stories of a resilient community. From the shadows of forced removals to the glow of emerging stars, it traces a journey of hardship, unity, and triumph. In the tapestry of Mamelodi's history, the threads of endurance weave a narrative of hope, defiance, and the unwavering spirit that shaped a legacy against the backdrop of apartheid's shadows.*

# Table of Contents

Foreword ..................................................... I
Prologue ..................................................... IV
Acknowledgments ..................................... VII
**Part One** .................................................. 1
Brief Background Of The Origin Of Mamelodi
Township ..................................................... 1
**Part Two** .................................................. 20
Letlapa ........................................................ 23
School Years .............................................. 27
Expulsion, 1976 Uprising And
Unemployment ......................................... 45
Journey Of Seeking Employment .............. 50
Later Years ................................................. 74
**Part Three** ................................................ 76
Maria And Selepe ...................................... 77
Brothel ....................................................... 88
Sermon ...................................................... 105
Confession ................................................. 111
Preparations .............................................. 118
Conversations ............................................ 126
Consequences Of The House Of Deceits .... 136
History Of Mamelodi ................................ 155
About The Author .................................... 158
Reference ................................................... 160

# FOREWORD

In the heart of the Mamelodi Township, a community shaped by the resilient spirit of its people unfolds in the pages that follow. This book delves into the rich tapestry of Mamelodi's history, where the echoes of forced relocations, apartheid's divisive policies, and the indomitable human spirit converge.

From the dusty landscapes that bore witness to the displacement of families from Vlakfontein Farm, Eastwood, Lady Selbourne, Riverside, and Sophia Town, the narrative unfolds like a melodic journey through time. Mamelodi, once known as Vlakfontein, emerged as a crucible of endurance, resilience, and communal strength.

The author navigates the reader through the township's early days, where families, separated by racial lines, found unity in shared struggles. Missionary schools, churches, and the emergence of African Initiated Churches played pivotal roles in shaping the spiritual landscape of Mamelodi. The imprint of a government's divisive "Divide and Rule" policy remains evident, fostering racial tension among residents and echoing the sentiments of a tumultuous era.

The narrative weaves through the fabric of daily life in Mamelodi—four-room houses, insufficient space for farming, and the prohibition of "shacks" in yards. The economic landscape, constrained yet vibrant, unfolds with stories of residents toiling in White Suburbs, pioneering businesses, and navigating the limitations imposed by an oppressive regime.

Amidst the challenges, the community flourished in education, sports, music, and various other endeavors. The introduction of television in 1976 coincided with the Soweto Uprising, underscoring a pivotal moment in South Africa's history.

As the pages turn, the reader is transported to a time when Mamelodi lacked basic services—no electrification, communal taps for water, and a bucket system for sewage. The intimate details of daily life—candles, paraffin lights, and the pervasive smoke from burning coal—paint a vivid picture of resilience in the face of adversity.

The narrative unfolds further, chronicling the establishment of schools, trade institutions, and communal spaces that became the heartbeat of Mamelodi. Yet, in the midst of progress, the specter of apartheid lingers, evident in the disparate treatment of Black and Coloured communities.

The author explores the intricate social fabric, where the City Council's attempt to regulate the consumption of alcohol led to a clash with the brewing traditions of Black women. This conflict, emblematic of broader struggles, became a focal point of resistance against oppressive laws.

The journey through Mamelodi's history culminates in the emergence of remarkable individuals who, against all odds, left an indelible mark on the community. From distance runners and musicians to educators and sports stars, Mamelodi became a crucible for nurturing talent and resilience.

As we embark on this literary exploration of Mamelodi's past, let us embrace the stories within these pages as testaments to the strength of the human spirit and the enduring power of community. May this book serve as a bridge between generations, preserving the legacy of Mamelodi and inspiring future chapters of resilience, unity, and triumph.

# PROLOGUE

This is the story of young individuals born and raised in the dusty area of Vlakfontein Township, later renamed Mamelodi Township. These youngsters hail from two contrasting socio-economic family backgrounds. Challenges in life know no boundaries; whether rich or poor, people are not immune to them.

These challenges may take on adversarial or non-adversarial forms in the later years of a person's life. The presence of challenging conditions has the potential to shape or shatter a person's future, particularly if one lacks an actionable plan to mitigate them.

Without a well-thought-out and actionable plan, challenges may cast their shadows over anyone, leaving them in a state of misery and stagnation. Each path presents unique challenges such as potholes, uneven surfaces, narrow stretches, and insufficient streetlights, along with hazards like spilled oil, posing threats to drivers.

Achieving the desired life outcomes requires commitment and sustainability. When faced with academic challenges, such as failing a subject, a prudent student does not succumb to defeat but instead initiates a thorough investigation to identify the reasons behind the failure.

This investigation may reveal issues like lack of preparation, inappropriate revision methods, or a misunderstanding of examination questions. Such insights provide a roadmap for overcoming the failure, guiding the student on how to study effectively and pass the subject.

However, if the student passes the subject, they will not discover the reasons for their success. Instead, they will accept the results as they are and move forward.

Challenges in life serve as the building blocks of success, requiring a well-thought-out and actionable plan to mitigate their impact.

This plan encompasses various elements, including but not limited to physical and mental fitness, perseverance, commitment, and focus.

For a mountain climber, the ultimate goal is to reach the summit. Achieving this objective demands a combination of physical and mental fitness, as well as unwavering focus and commitment.

In preparation for the climb, the climber typically dedicates several weeks, if not months, to physical training, maintaining a balanced diet, and other related activities.

Challenges don't prescribe specific actions or management strategies for individuals. Instead, they possess the potential to shape and mold a person, steering them towards the accomplishment of their desired personal goals.

# ACKNOWLEDGMENTS

In crafting this narrative, I am indebted to the resilient community of Mamelodi Township, whose stories form the heart and soul of this book. To the individuals who generously shared their memories, struggles, and triumphs, thank you for entrusting me with the privilege of documenting your history.

Special appreciation goes to the families who, despite the challenges of forced relocations and racial segregation, held onto their traditions and dreams. Your resilience and determination to build a life in the face of adversity are both inspiring and humbling.

I extend my gratitude to the educators, community leaders, and unsung heroes who, against the backdrop of an oppressive system, nurtured education, sports, music, and various forms of self-expression. Your contributions to the cultural fabric of Mamelodi are immeasurable.

This work would not have been possible without the meticulous research conducted by scholars such as Walker & Van Der

Waal and the insightful observations made by Machaba. Their dedication to preserving the history of Mamelodi has paved the way for a deeper understanding of the township's evolution.

I would also like to acknowledge the broader context of South Africa's history, acknowledging the struggles and triumphs of the nation as a whole. The complexities of apartheid, resistance, and transformation have shaped the narrative, and I am grateful for the opportunity to contribute to the ongoing conversation.

To the memory of those who resisted injustice and fought for a better future, your legacy lives on in the pages of this book. Lastly, a heartfelt thank you to my support system—family, friends, and mentors—who provided encouragement, guidance, and unwavering belief in the importance of sharing stories that resonate with the human experience.

May this book serve as a tribute to the rich tapestry of Mamelodi's history and a testament to the indomitable spirit of its people.

# Part One

# BRIEF BACKGROUND OF THE ORIGIN OF MAMELODI TOWNSHIP

## 1. ORIGIN

Several socio-economic and political factors played a role in the establishment of Mamelodi Township. One reason was the need to relocate people from areas designated for a specific race or to areas close to industries requiring labor. The process of relocation varied; sometimes, there was consultation beforehand, while other times, people were moved without much say, resembling a herd of cattle.

In the case of Vlakfontein Area, people from different regions were forcefully relocated. Blacks were moved from Vlakfontein Farm, Eastwood (now Garsfontein, a White suburb), Lady Selbourne (now Pretoria Gardens, another White suburb), Riverside, and Sophia Town. The Pretoria City Council purchased parts 2 & 3 of the Vlakfontein 3293 R Farmland to create a Black Urban Area, as documented by Walker & Van Der Waal in 1991.

The establishment of the Vlakfontein Urban Area began with the construction of 16 houses in 1951, according to Machaba. In 1953, the urban area underwent a name change and became Mamelodi Township. The residents chose this name in homage to President Paul Kruger of the South African Republic, also known as Transvaal. They associated him with the ability to whistle and imitate birds, leading to the name "Mamelodi," which translates to "Mother of Melodies."

Even today, many residents still refer to Mamelodi as "Vlak," while some use the abbreviation "Mams." The history of Mamelodi Township reflects a complex interplay of social, economic, and political forces that shaped its formation and naming.

## 2. HOUSES

In the beginning, the houses were simple four-room structures, with bare walls and uncovered floors. After 1976, some politicians dubbed these homes "Matchboxes." During the 1994 general elections, they promised to build better houses if they won. The elections came and went, giving birth to what became known as RDP Houses. However, these new houses were only half the size of the original four-room houses.

Despite their small size, RDP Houses could house families of six to eight members. Sleeping arrangements were tight: parents in one bedroom, girls in another, and boys in both the dining room and the kitchen. The government, in an effort to control housing, prohibited the construction of "shacks" or tin houses in yards unless they were brick garages or exterior rooms.

Yards were cramped, offering little space for growing crops or raising animals, unlike the more spacious rural Vlakfontein. The government's strategy of "Divide and Rule" aimed to prevent residents from uniting against them, turning them into racial enemies. Residents were segregated into different sections based on their race, such as grouping Northern Sotho and Tswana-speaking people together, Tsongas and Vendas together, and Ngunis (Ndebeles, Zulus, and Xhosas) together.

Unfortunately, things got tense among the folks in Mamelodi due to a not-so-great arrangement. The government at the time, the National Party, had some not-so-friendly names for the Black community like Naturelle, Kaffirs, Non-Whites, Plurals, and simply Blacks.

Adding to the separation, Coloureds had their own area named Eersterust, located on the opposite side of Mamelodi. This township, Mamelodi, was split into two parts by a river—Mamelodi East and Mamelodi West.

Zooming into Mamelodi West, the house numbers and sections went through a makeover when Vlakfontein became part of Mamelodi Township.

The numbering system kicked off with the first house in the first street of section A, starting with the cool number 1, and continuing from there.

| Vlakfontein Sections | Mamelodi Sections |
|---|---|
| A4 | Section A |

| A1 | Section B |
| --- | --- |
| A3 | Section C |
| B1 | Section D |
| B2 | Section E |
| B3 | Section F |
| C1 | Section G |
| C2 | Section H |
| C3 | Section J |
| C4 | Section k |
| C5 | Section L |
| D1 | Section M |
| D2 | Section N |
| D3 | Section P |
| D4 | Section Q |

**Mamelodi East Section**

In Mamelodi East, houses are like secret codes with five magical numbers. The first two, like 12, 13, or 14, are like the names of the sections – the special places that give each house its own identity. The other three numbers are the cool kids called "Mazakhele" and "Kalambazo."

Now, picture this: Mamelodi East and Mamelodi West are like best friends separated by the Moretele River. They share stories across the water, but each has its own adventures.

But wait, there's more! In the later years, two new sections, U & V, joined the neighborhood. Tsakane section became the cool hangout spot. Over in Mamelodi West, there are the Moretele houses, standing tall. Meanwhile, in Mamelodi East, there's the awesome Ikageng section and the green paradise called Mamelodi Gardens.

So, in this land of numbers and sections, the houses have their own tales to tell, and each one is like a chapter in the story of Mamelodi.

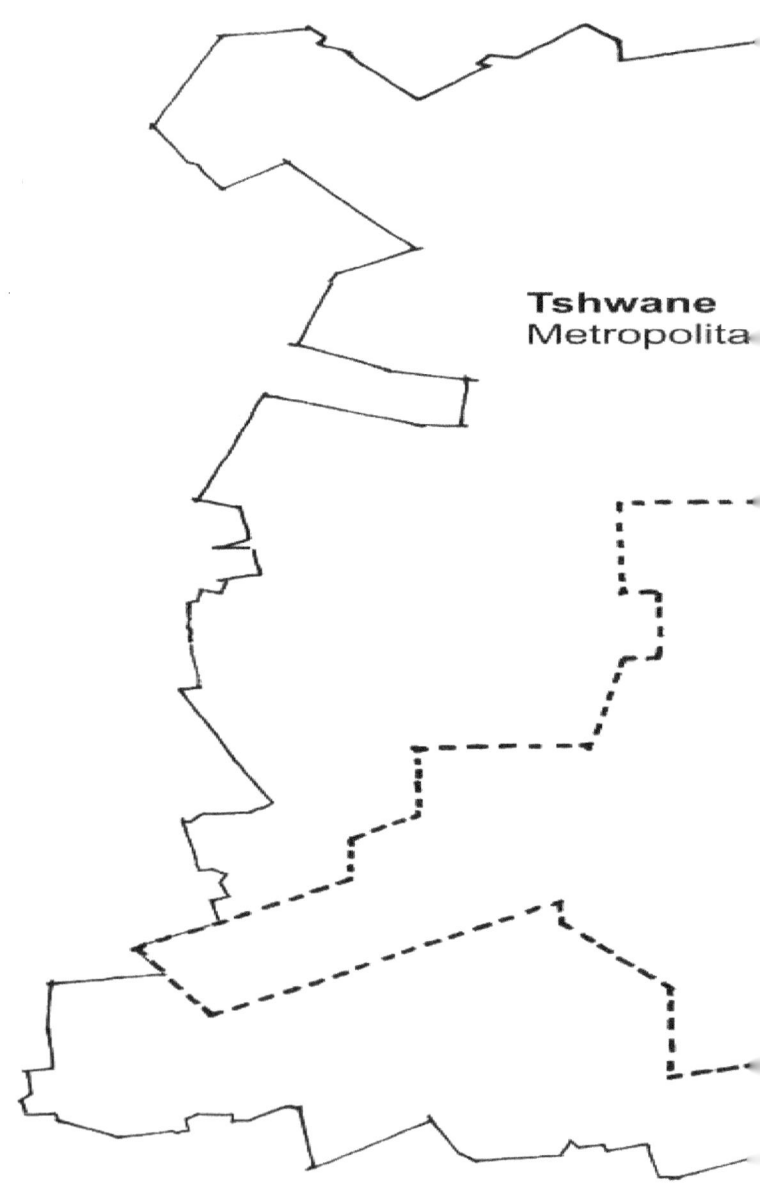

**Tshwane**
Metropolita

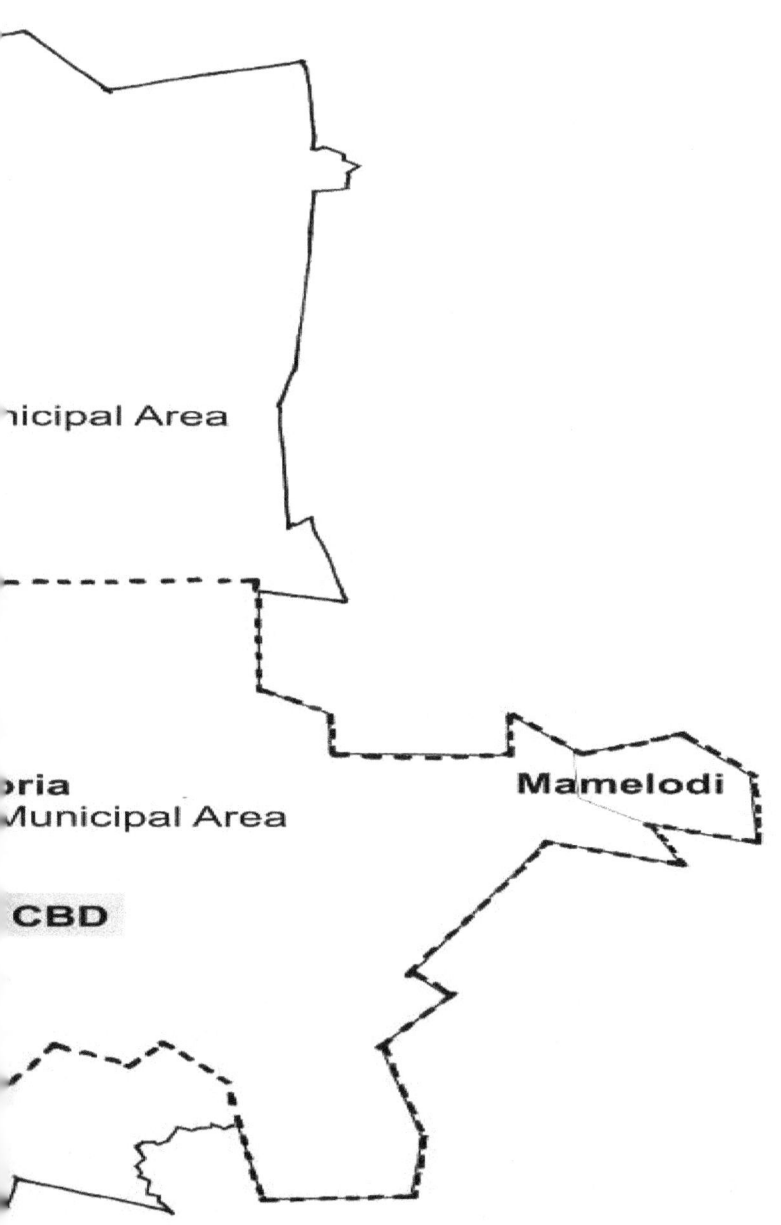

By D. Schoulund 2010 adapted from IDP,1999.

Mamelodi Township is situated North-East of Pretoria and is about 24.6 Km from Pretoria.

## 3. SERVICE DELIVERY

Houses stood in neat rows, but the roads beneath were not paved. The absence of electricity cast shadows over the township, leaving it reliant on communal six-taps stationed at the heart of each street. These taps drew water from an elevated tank, creating a shared source for the entire community.

Mamelodi remained untouched by the glow of electrification. Instead, homes were illuminated by the soft flicker of candles and paraffin lights. Cooking unfolded with the warmth of coal-braziers and the steady hum of paraffin primus stoves, bringing sustenance and boiled water to the residents.

As the sun dipped into the horizon, the air in Mamelodi became veiled in smoke from burning coal, painting the afternoons in a unique hue. Within the modest interiors, candles and paraffin lights fought against the encroaching darkness.

The township grappled with the absence of a modern sewage system. In its place, the bucket system took charge, requiring the City Council to enlist individuals from distant provinces. These anonymous workers, their faces concealed, became known as "Bo Mambongane," a term coined by the residents, signifying those who bear the burden of waste.

## 4. LEGISLATIONS

The government brought in a bunch of rules to control black people. They had to carry this thing called a "Dom pass" all the time – it's like an inside passport. This pass showed that the person was allowed to be in the area and had a job.

If someone didn't have a job, they could get arrested for being unemployed, which they called "Lofer skaap" in Afrikaans. Even students had to carry this pass around. There were different sections on the stamp, like section 10 (A), which told where the person was born, like in Pretoria or a rural area.

Then there were these local cops known as "Plaat Keps" or "Flat Hat" because, you guessed it, their hats were flat on top. They wore khaki uniforms and their job was to check and arrest people without jobs.

If anyone visited Mamelodi, they had to go to the police station and let them know. The police would give them a paper saying it's okay to visit, showing who they were visiting and for how long. On the last day of the visit, the police would check if the person had gone back home; if not, they'd get arrested.

To make matters worse, the government had all these mean names for black people, like calling them "Natives," "Kaffirs," "Non-Whites," "Plurals," and just plain "Blacks."

PROTOTYPE: EMPLOYMENT STATUS IN A DOMPASS.

|  | Informa |
|  | Sc |
|  | Permission |
| Name of Employer | Month & Year | Signature ( Employee |
| ABCD Enterprise | April 1961 | ✍ |

| garding: | | |
| --- | --- | --- |
| 0. | | |
| in the Area | | |
| mployment Status | Date Discharged | Signature of Employer |
| Employed | | |

Moreover, the Dom Pass was like a key for Black people, and Coloureds held a book of life.

## PERMIT TO VISIT MAMELODI

## 5. COMMUNICATION SYSTEM

Once upon a time, the General Post Office (GPO), now known as the South African Post Office, was like the hub of all things communication and more. It was the go-to place for making phone calls, sending and receiving mail, paying rent, and even sending telegrams. People could also save their money there.

Back in those days, there were landline phones, but radios hadn't made their debut yet. Then, in 1960, the Radio Bantu came into the scene, though it had a limited broadcast time from 9:00 to 11:00.

If you stepped inside the GPO, you'd find two large photos of White Males in a single frame, each one telling a different story. On one side, there was a plump man comfortably seated, holding a cigar and surrounded by paper money on his desk. Below this image was a message in Afrikaans – "U het ge Spaar" (One has saved). On the other side, there was a white male looking distressed, holding his head and wearing torn clothes, accompanied by a message – "U het nie ge Spaar nie" (One has not saved). It was a visual reminder of the importance of saving money.

## 6. SOCIAL LIFE

In a place where comfort was a distant dream, children found joy in the simple pleasures of dusty roads. They played timeless games like Morabaraba, a strategic board game for two, jumped to the rhythm of rope-skipping, and disappeared and reappeared in the excitement of hide and seek.

But this quaint charm masked a darker side. The absence of basic facilities and the divisive force of racial segregation gave rise to a slew of illicit activities in the townships. Houses spiraled into chaos with illegal break-ins, and the streets echoed with the unsettling shadows of crimes like robbery and assault, especially in the evening hours. Gangs flourished, marking their presence with loud Stok vel parties that blared music from afternoon till the dead of night. Among the chaos, there were flashy displays of designer clothes, symbols of a world far removed from the struggles of everyday life.

Many residents were strangers to urban life, grappling with its demands. Survival meant venturing into the White Suburbs for work, with women taking up roles as domestic workers and men toiling as gardeners and laborers in factories and companies. Life was a delicate balance between the innocence of children's games and the harsh realities that awaited them in the unforgiving townships.

## 7. ECONOMIC CONDITIONS

Once upon a time, South Africa danced to the tune of the British government. They used Pounds and Pennies as their money. Then in 1961, South Africa broke free from British rule, shouting, "Hello independence!" and became the Republic of South Africa (RSA) under the National Party Government.

On the 14th of February in that year, the Brits' Pounds and Pennies were kicked out, and in marched the Rand and Cents. The Rand got its name from the Witwatersrand region, a place where gold popped up like it was saying, "Here I am!"

The paper money sported the face of Jan Van Riebeck, a guy who must have been quite famous. There were also ships on the money, boats from the Dutch Indian Company in Holland. These ships were sailing to the East for spices, but a wild storm had other plans. On April 5, 1652, they got tossed to the Cape of Point. That day used to be a big deal, a public holiday, until the African National Congress took over in 1994 and said, "No more holiday, folks."

Back in the day, life wasn't all city lights and skyscrapers. People weren't used to the hustle and bustle of city living. Many had a tough time just trying to get by. If you wanted to make some cash, you had to roll up your sleeves and work in the White Suburbs. Women took on the role of domestic workers, while the men tried their hands at gardening or worked in factories and companies. It was a real grind, but that's how the Rand rolled.

Residents took on various initiatives to boost their income. In those days, there were no "Spaza-shops" (small informal stores) or "Shebeens" (places where people bought alcoholic beverages and enjoyed music and dancing).

Business opportunities were scarce, and the most common ventures involved selling coal and wood for stoves, offering vegetables for sale, making and selling "fat-cakes," and earning extra money by plastering the interior walls of homes.

**The primary lucrative businesses included:**

- Selling coal and firewood for braziers and stoves.

- Providing paraffin for primus stoves and lights.

• Black Shops, established by the City Council, offered a diverse range of merchandise and even extended credit to families.

## 8. EDUCATION SYSTEM

Before Bantu Education came into play, most schools for black students were run by missions with some state support. Then, in 1953, the government introduced the Bantu Education Act, a move that wasn't welcomed by the people. This new system aimed to ensure that black children learned only what the government deemed useful for its agenda.

As a result, some mission schools faced closure in 1962, compelled by the government's declaration of their locations as "white areas." Take Kilnerton School in Weaving Park, Pretoria, for example; it had to shut down because Weaving Park was now designated as a "White Area."

In 1955, a response to this educational shift was the establishment of Vlakfontein Industrial School, a trade school. This institution offered a range of disciplines including carpentry, watchmaking, bricklaying, electricity, and typing. The landscape of education was changing, shaped by policies that influenced not just what was taught, but also where it could be taught.

Back in 1955, they added a new school to the mix – Mamelodi Secondary School. As time rolled on, more schools joined the party. Then came the Municipality Library, Community Halls, a Cinema, and a Maternity House.

Fast forward to 1976, and guess what popped up on screens? Television! But that year wasn't just about new channels. It was also when the whole country faced the June 1976 saga, famously known as the Soweto Uprising. Students took to the streets, not because they were auditioning for a parade but to protest the not-so-cool use of Afrikaans and Bantu Education in Black schools.

The protest had its moments, and the struggle didn't go unnoticed. It paved the way for lifting the ban on Political Parties. Jump to 1994, and the country threw a big party – the first-ever inclusive general election for a democratic government. And just like that, a new chapter began.

### 9. TRANSPORT

Getting from Mamelodi to Pretoria CBC was a journey filled with choices: trains, buses, or taxis were the main players in this transportation tale.

There were two train stations along the way—Denneboom (which translates to Pine Tree in Afrikaans) and Eerste Fabriek (Afrikaans for First Factory). The latter, initially known as Eerste Fabriek Hatherly Distillers, had its grand opening on the 5th of July in 1883, courtesy of President Paul Kruger (source: Kaye, 1978, p4-30).

### 10. SPORT FACILITIES

There weren't fancy sports places. Schools did sports right there on their own grounds. Football happened on a ground without any grass.

A real stadium only showed up in the late 1970s. Guess what? They called it Mr. Hezekiel Mothiba Pitjie, the first Mayor's name. Cool, right?

## 11.   NOTABLE PEOPLE

Amidst the challenges and oppressive apartheid laws, a host of remarkable individuals emerged, making their mark in various fields such as education, politics, sports, soccer, boxing, athletics, and music.

**Here are a few notable figures:**

•   Benoni Malaka: A standout long-distance runner with an athletic prowess.

•   Dr. Phillip Tabane: The visionary founder of the Malombo Musical band, clinching victory at the Orlando Music Festival in 1964.

• Samson Ndhazi: A bodybuilder who graced the pages of She and True Africa magazines.

• Motuba: An educator who not only imparted knowledge but also composed music, earning recognition in school music competitions.

• Vusi Mahlasela: A musical talent who left an indelible mark in the world of music.

- Don Laka: A maestro in Jazz music.

- Soccer Stars: Including Jan Lichaba, Motale, Themba Mnguni, Edward Motale, and Joel Masilela.

- George Masango: A skilled boxer who showcased prowess in the ring.

- Aubrey Masango: A voice on the radio, making waves as a radio presenter.

- Manana Phetla and Phillemon Tefo: Distinguished politicians.

- Freedom Fighters: Dr. Fabien Riebero, Ntladi Moseka, and Solomon Mahlangu, who fought valiantly for freedom.

The characters in Part Two and Part Three were born and raised in the dusty landscapes of Mamelodi, tightly controlled by the National Party Government. Their parents endured the hardships imposed by the apartheid regime. However, through unwavering dedication and commitment, these parents succeeded in nurturing their children into individuals of substance, defying the odds stacked against them.

# Part Two

# CHAPTER 1

## Letlapa

Letlapa's roots were firmly planted in Mamelodi, a place his parents once called home on Vlakfontein Farm. Despite their Eagle family being financially and educationally modest, they possessed an innate curiosity for learning and embracing new ideas. Their determination led them to acquire new skills, propelling them toward their aspirations.

Their main objectives were simple yet profound: nurture and care for their children, instill moral values, and ensure education. These ambitions were deeply embedded in the minds of their offspring. As the years unfolded, their children evolved into individuals of exemplary character and education.

Letlapa, the youngest among six siblings, experienced a typical boyhood, playing on the dusty streets and participating in communal games like Morabaraba, a traditional two-player

# CHAPTER 1

strategy board game, rope-skipping, and hide and seek.

Letlapa's mother hailed from Ellisrus Farm, now part of Lephalale Local Municipality in the north-western Waterberg District of the Limpopo Province. Meanwhile, his father originated from Mozambique. Fate brought his parents together in Johannesburg, where they later settled on Vlakfontein Farm after being uprooted from Sophiatown, a community demolished by the government.

In the aftermath, the residents of Vlakfontein Farm underwent relocation to the Vlakfontein Urban Area, subsequently evolving into Mamelodi Township.

Life in our town was tough, especially on the financial front. There just weren't enough opportunities to make money. Many men found themselves working as migrant laborers, while women took up jobs as domestic workers in the affluent White Suburbs. The strain on families was evident – broken homes became the norm, and countless children, including Letlapa, grew up without their fathers around.

Letlapa's mother, determined to make ends meet, delved into various money-making ventures. On weekends, before heading to church, and on days when she wasn't at her regular job, she would bake and sell "Fat Cakes" – a tasty treat that became a small source of income.

But that wasn't all. She also engaged in a unique game called "Fafi" or "Mo China," albeit an illegal one. In this game, numbers between 1 and 36 were involved, and each day, one number was excluded. Punters would bet on a number or numbers by placing their bets in numbered bags. At the end of the month, one punter was responsible for collecting these bags and delivering them to Mo China, who, in return, would provide a winning number. Those lucky bags containing the correct number would then be rewarded with a payout.

In a challenging socio-economic environment, Letlapa's family found creative and sometimes unconventional ways to navigate the difficulties they faced, showcasing resilience and resourcefulness in their pursuit of a better life.

**Each number, had a meaning:**

| Number | Meaning | Number | Meaning |
| --- | --- | --- | --- |
| 1 | King | 19 | Girls |
| 2 | Monkey | 20 | Cat |
| 3 | Big water/Ocean/Sea | 21 | Elephant |
| 4 | Dead person | 22 | Ship |
| 5 | Tiger | 23 | Horse |
| 6 | Cow | 24 | Big mouth |
| 7 | Thief | 25 | Big house |
| 8 | Pig | 26 | Soldiers |
| 9 | Moon | 27 | Dog |
| 10 | Eggs | 28 | Small fish |
| 11 | Car | 29 | Small water |
| 12 | Old woman | 30 | Priest |
| 13 | Small fish | 31 | Fire |

# CHAPTER 1

| 14 | Dead person | 32 | Big money/ Gold |
| --- | --- | --- | --- |
| 15 | Prostitute | 33 | Boys |
| 16 | Doves | 34 | Feacies |
| 17 | White woman | 35 | Male private part |
| 18 | Small money | 36 | Female private part |

Letlapa helped his mom by going to people's homes to talk about betting. His dad worked for a construction company that built schools and universities in different places in South Africa. His dad knew how to do a lot of things like painting, plastering, and laying bricks. They called him a "Jack of All Trades, Master of None."

When he had time off, he made extra money by building garages for people, putting in big windows, and painting houses. The extra money helped the family take care of some important things at home during the holidays.

# Chapter 2

## SCHOOL YEARS

**Lower Primary School**

In 1963, Letlapa, a spirited eight-year-old, embarked on his educational journey at Vulamehlo, a nearby Lower Primary School that beckoned him to "open your eyes." Nestled just a five-minute stroll from his home, it became the haven of his budding dreams.

Unlike some peers who kick-started their learning escapades at Pre-school (Creche), Letlapa's narrative took a different turn. His parents, grappling with financial constraints, couldn't af-

# CHAPTER 2

ford the fees for a Pre-school education.

Yet, Letlapa was a pint-sized powerhouse – physically robust, well-behaved, devoid of aggression, and brimming with curiosity. His mother, thoroughly impressed by his demeanor, decided to elevate his joy and commendable behavior by gifting him a pair of splendid school shoes.

These shoes had a unique origin. A local man, having procured them for his own son, faced an unexpected hiccup. The shoes, intended for the son, turned out to be oversized, and the store where they were purchased refused to exchange them for the correct size.

Enter Letlapa's stage. After a day at school, he returned home to a delightful surprise – the very shoes his mother had acquired from the local man. Letlapa's face radiated happiness, as these shoes not only adorned his feet but also symbolized a mother's unwavering love, resourcefulness, and commitment to her son's bright future.

The next day, Letlapa eagerly headed to school with his brand-new shoes, hoping to show them off to his classmates. However, his excitement was short-lived.

As Letlapa sat in his classroom, a sudden interruption unfolded. A police officer and a man in handcuffs appeared at the door, seeking the attention of his teacher.

"Hello, Teacher!" greeted the policeman, stationed at the classroom entrance where Letlapa was seated.

Curious, the teacher approached the door. "Hello, sir. Can I help you?" she inquired.

"Yes, Teacher. The Principal informed me that the student I'm looking for is in your classroom. His name is Letlapa. Is he in your class?" asked the policeman.

The teacher, slightly concerned, replied, "Yes, sir. Has he done something wrong?" she questioned, a hint of worry in her voice.

"Not really. Please call him outside. I need to ask him some questions," the policeman requested, conveying the message from the police.

The teacher hurried back into the classroom and beckoned Letlapa to step outside. Curious whispers spread among the other students: "What did Letlapa do?" Their gaze shifted to a police officer and a man in handcuffs standing outside, visible through the windows.

"Hey there, young man. Is your name Letlapa?" inquired the police officer.

Breathing heavily, Letlapa replied, "Yes."

"Do you know this man?" the police officer continued.

"No, I saw him near a house close to ours, maybe two or three days ago," Letlapa explained.

## CHAPTER 2

The officer probed further, "What was he carrying?"

"He had a small box," Letlapa answered.

Curious about the box, the police officer pressed, "What kind of box?"

"I can't recall the size," Letlapa admitted.

The officer then presented a shoebox and asked, "Is this the same?"

"Yes," Letlapa confirmed, still catching his breath.

"Did you see what was inside that box?" the police officer questioned.

"No, he talked to my mother, gave her the box, and left," Letlapa responded.

The officer glanced at Letlapa's shoes and asked, "Are these the shoes your mother bought for you?"

"Yes," Letlapa affirmed.

Are these the shoes you sold to this boy's mother?" the police asked the man in handcuffs.

"Yeah," the man grunted in response.

# SCHOOL YEARS

"Sorry, teacher, but I have to take these shoes from Letlapa. This guy stole them from a local store and sold them to Letlapa's mom," the police explained.

The police instructed Letlapa to take off the shoes, thanked the teacher for her cooperation, and left with both the stolen shoes and the handcuffed man.

Letlapa had no idea that his mom had bought stolen shoes, and his mom was clueless about their questionable origin. The realization hit Letlapa hard, and he began crying uncontrollably.

"Don't worry, my boy. It's not your fault," the teacher comforted him.

Letlapa continued sobbing as the principal arrived and spoke with the teacher. Eventually, the teacher told Letlapa to go home, and fortunately, his house was just around the corner. When he arrived home barefoot and in tears, his mother was shocked by the unexpected sight.

After school, Letlapa's pals dropped by his place.

"Hey, did the cops really nab your new kicks at school?" inquired Kolobe.

"Yeah," replied Letlapa.

"Why?" questioned Sam.

## CHAPTER 2

"They claimed they were stolen," Letlapa explained.

"Did your mom know they were stolen when she got them?" Rose wondered.

"I don't know," Letlapa admitted.

"Whoa, that's awkward," commented Kolobe.

As they were leaving, Letlapa's class teacher walked in.

"Hey, I appreciate your support for Letlapa," the teacher said to them.

"Thanks, Teacher," they replied before heading out.

The teacher had a chat with Letlapa's mom, explaining the whole incident.

"Were you aware that the shoes were stolen?" the teacher asked.

"No, I had no idea," Letlapa's mom replied.

"We need to be careful when buying stuff from people, even if we know them," the teacher advised.

"I won't make that mistake again," the mother assured the teacher.

# SCHOOL YEARS

"I only got them to reward his good behavior; little did I know it would bring him misery."

"Okay, don't blame yourself," the teacher reassured. "We learn a lot from failure than from success," she added, emphasizing it was a valuable lesson meant to be shared with other parents.

For a week, Letlapa hesitated to return to school, fearing the embarrassment and teasing from fellow students. Yet, understanding the challenges at Letlapa's home, the compassionate teacher rallied support from colleagues, raising funds to buy him a pair of shoes identical to the ones that had caused him distress.

This act of kindness spurred Letlapa to overcome his reluctance and resume his studies. With newfound motivation, he excelled in Lower Primary School, proving that the laughter of those who mock your struggles can fuel determination.

**People who laugh at your misery, their laughter make you more determined.**

### Higher Primary School

Advancing to Higher Primary School in 1967, Letlapa successfully completed his primary education in 1970. The journey continued into High School at Mamelodi High School, where he became the first in his family to reach Matric (Grade 12).

### High School

## CHAPTER 2

High school life was vibrant with various sports activities, and each student had to participate in one. Letlapa chose to engage in debate, a formal discussion with opposing sides, and joined the Boys Choir. These experiences not only enriched his academic journey but also shaped him into a well-rounded individual.

Friday afternoons meant lively debates at school. The rule was clear: jackets and ties were a must. Letlapa found himself in a predicament as he lacked a school blazer. Undeterred, he swiped his brother's black jacket the day before the debate, not bothering to ask for permission.

Post-debate, instead of heading straight home, Letlapa decided to flaunt his borrowed attire. To his dismay, his brother was already home when he arrived. The jacket's unauthorized excursion triggered his brother's anger, serving as a valuable lesson for Letlapa—never take someone's clothes without permission.

As Letlapa navigated adolescence, he embraced a newfound adventurous spirit. His peers were dipping their toes into the world of teenage romance, and those without a special someone faced mockery. Letlapa, with three loyal friends—Kolobe, Tau, and Sam—was no exception.

After the school bell rang, Letlapa shed his uniform, disappearing into the world only to resurface at home late in the evening. The journey through adolescence had begun, marked by lessons in borrowing, the complexities of friendship, and the allure of the unknown.

# SCHOOL YEARS

Salome had a side hustle selling beer to a specific group. While she was busy with work, Letlapa and his pals sneakily swiped a beer or two, emptied them, filled them with water, sealed the bottles, and discreetly returned them to the fridge.

This mischief almost wrecked his mom's business when some customers suspected something fishy and complained that the bottles contained water instead of beer. It dawned on Letlapa that he was like a tree with feeble roots. His ventures didn't pan out as expected, so he changed his tune and started putting more effort into his studies.

Unfortunately, many students were getting into trouble, leading to some getting expelled for disrespecting teachers and fighting with their peers. Meanwhile, the police were on their toes, with patrol cars chasing after criminals regularly. Sirens echoed in the distance, marking the constant hustle of the police force.

In the neighborhood, there was a playful saying:

"If you spot a Black man sprinting, he's dodging the police.

"If you catch a Coloured Man in a hurry, he's probably headed to the liquor store."

"If a White man is rushing, he's likely running late for a meeting."

Parents faced challenges urging their kids to go to school, concentrate on studies, and avoid getting involved with gangs.

CHAPTER 2

*The beginning of a journey is the start of self-reliance and manhood.*

## Money Generating Initiatives

Letlapa felt the influence of his friends and decided to explore various ways to make money. He wanted to get the stylish clothes his friends had and also help his family buy some food.

### Peanuts, Sweets Apples And Liquor Vendor

Letlapa and his friends loved to get creative with their snacks. They would buy mini packs of peanuts and a mix of sweets from Indian shops in Marabastad. Then, they'd combine these treats and repackage them into small plastic bags.

In Marabastad, the trains from Pretoria Station took passengers to different destinations like Atteridgeville, Mamelodi, or Pietersburg. The train carriages were divided into three classes: First Class for Whites, Second Class for some elites, and Third Class for Blacks. The Third Class carriages were always crowded, with South African Railways Police keeping a watchful eye.

Interestingly, there were two categories of railway police: Black officers for the Third Class carriages and White officers for the First Class carriages. The White officers, known as "Gunmen," carried guns, while the Black officers did not.

Despite the risks involved, Letlapa and his friends sold their snacks to passengers on trains moving from Pretoria Station to Eerstefabriek Station in Mamelodi. The South African Railway

Policemen on the trains would sometimes arrest them and confiscate their goods. Nevertheless, the venture was quite profitable.

During the long Good Friday and Christmas holidays, Letlapa expanded his sales to trains transporting people to their homes or visiting their families in places like Limpopo, Zimbabwe, and Mozambique. It added an extra layer of excitement and challenge to their entrepreneurial adventure.

Passengers on the train were more into booze, but buying and selling it for a profit was pricey. Letlapa and his buddies came up with a crafty plan—they started selling pretend brandy, a popular drink at the time.

Their fake brandy was a mix of twenty percent spirit and eighty percent sifted black tea. They poured this concoction into bottles with brandy labels and passed it off as the real deal. To make it convincing, they even let potential buyers taste the actual brandy.

This scheme was risky because if someone figured out it wasn't real, trouble could follow. To stay a step ahead, they always wore two shirts. After making a sale, they hopped off at the next station, hit the restroom, changed shirts, put on a cap, and waited for the next train home.

### Caddie

Letlapa decided to make some extra cash by lugging golf bags around at the local golf course. It seemed like a pretty safe gig,

## CHAPTER 2

and the pay was good. However, the money he earned from being a caddie turned out to be so tempting that it distracted him from his schoolwork.

The golf course, where Letlapa worked, was situated in a predominantly white neighborhood. On the greens, you'd find all sorts of golfers, from beginners trying to get the hang of it to seasoned pros showing off their skills. Interestingly, though, all the golfers were white.

If you were a pro, you were lucky enough to have a caddie like Letlapa carrying your golf bag. But if you were just starting out in the golfing world, well, you were on your own—no caddies for the amateur golfers.

**Coal Vendor**

Letlapa snagged a weekend gig peddling coal. Picture this: a horse-drawn cart trundling through the streets, Letlapa and his mates perched on it, hollering "A malahle-Malahle" (Coal-Coal) to lure in potential buyers.

One day, as luck would have it, the cart rolled down Letlapa's own street. Unaware that her son was part of the coal-selling crew, his mother halted the cart and ordered a tin of coal. To her surprise, out stepped Letlapa, covered in coal dust, sporting tattered clothes, ready to deliver the goods.

Undeterred by his sooty appearance, he hoisted the coal-filled tin onto his shoulder and marched it home. Despite the gritty exterior, Letlapa remained unfazed.

# SCHOOL YEARS

However, his mother couldn't shake off the discomfort of seeing her child in such a job. Come afternoon, she gently urged him to ditch the coal-selling venture. Reluctantly, Letlapa complied, but an insatiable yearning to unearth a money-making venture still bubbled within him.

**traditional healer/ sangoma**

Letlapa's brother would get this interesting leaflet about special medicines all the way from Kwa-Zulu Natal. The pamphlet was like a magical menu, suggesting remedies for things like good luck or money.

Back then, everyone really looked up to Sangomas, these special healers with ancient wisdom. No matter what job you had, people would go to them for help. They were like the go-to experts for everything – keeping bad spirits away, getting strong potions, and even helping women who wanted to have babies.

One chilly day in September, Letlapa was just sitting on the porch, feeling cold even though the sun was shining. His mom got a bit worried seeing him shiver like that in the heat. So, she decided to take him to a nearby Sangoma, hoping they had a remedy for whatever was bothering him.

The Sangoma led Letlapa into her special room, called Domba. Before stepping inside, they both removed their shoes and left them outside. Inside the room, a grass mat awaited them. The Sangoma, Letlapa, and the person who brought Letlapa all took their places on the mat. Then, either Letlapa or the accompanying person placed the consulting fee on the mat.

# CHAPTER 2

The Sangoma took out bones from a small bag made of skin, holding them in hand. With a gentle request, the Sangoma asked Letlapa to exhale onto the bones and then toss them onto the grass mat. Following this ritual, the Sangoma asked both Letlapa and the accompanying person to nod in agreement, saying, "Se ya vuma" – signaling their shared understanding.

The Sangoma shook her head, glanced at Letlapa's mother, and declared that he was under a spell due to his intelligence at school. To dispel this malevolent spirit, Letlapa needed to undergo a "steam bath" and sustain himself for two days on the meat of a white chicken along with prescribed medicine. The mother, with a nod, agreed to the remedy.

Letlapa was led into a sizable bath filled with hot stones, hot water, and a concoction of healing herbs. Covered tightly by a blanket held by other Sangomas, the steam grew oppressively hot for Letlapa. In an unexpected turn, he managed to poke a hole in the blanket and sprinted home wearing only a trunk.

The Sangomas pursued him, but he dashed into his room, locking the door behind him. Despite his mother's pleas, he remained silent. Eventually, the Sangomas gave up and departed.

The next day, aided by a friend, Letlapa sought the advice of a medical doctor. It turned out he was suffering from gonorrhea. The doctor provided medication and recommended circumcision. Within two weeks, Letlapa recuperated and underwent the procedure at a hospital. Since then, he has remained free from any sexually transmitted diseases.

**Traditional Medicine Pamphlet**

One day, Letlapa discovered a pamphlet on his table showcasing various traditional medicines. One particular remedy caught his eye, claiming that by touching someone, their money would magically transfer to him. Intrigued, he decided to order it and headed to the Post Office.

In just a week, a parcel arrived for him from the General Post Office. Inside were three small packages labeled "Number-One, Number Two, and Number Three." Excitedly, Letlapa read the instructions.

Package number one instructed him to wash his body with its contents, and he followed through. Package number two required him to mix its contents with water, drink, and induce vomiting, which he also completed.

However, the final package, number three, demanded a peculiar task. Letlapa had to walk naked in the middle of the night to a cemetery, gather soil from any grave, mix it with the package's contents, and scatter the mixture at a crossroads.

# CHAPTER 2

Fearful of being mistaken for a witch and facing potential harm, Letlapa hesitated. Eventually, he decided not to carry out the last step, opting to discard the package instead of risking his safety in the eerie night.

**Drummer**

Letlapa not only drummed with American beats at a nearby Ballroom and Latin music hub but also added rhythm to the local celebrations. The tunes were mostly for those who loved to dance, yet there were also melodies for special moments like weddings and graduation ceremonies.

**Gardner**

Letlapa decided to try his hand at gardening in the White Suburbs. On his first day, he noticed something unusual. As he arrived for work, he spotted a dog munching on a meal. Curious, he observed from a distance and realized it was the same dish he usually had for breakfast.

To his surprise, the housekeeper collected the dish from the dog, cleaned it, and, after a short while, served Letlapa his breakfast in the same dish. Perplexed, he asked the housekeeper if it was indeed the same dish the dog had used, and she confirmed it.

Feeling disrespected and dehumanized, Letlapa decided to quit the gardening job on the spot. Since that day, he swore off any garden work. Unfortunately, this decision didn't bring him joy; instead, it added to the pain and unhappiness he felt. His

# SCHOOL YEARS

schoolwork suffered as a result, as he spent more time avoiding assignments and chores.

**Letlapa and Girlfriend**

Around three years before Letlapa wrote his final Grade 12 examination, he met his girlfriend. At that time, she was attending the nearby Higher Primary School. The following year, she moved on to a Secondary School.

A year before Letlapa completed Grade 12, his girlfriend became pregnant and gave birth to a girl eight months prior to his graduation. In January 1976, their daughter was nine months old. Fortunately, Letlapa didn't feel the pressure of sole responsibility, as his sister and aunt were supporting them.

In August 1978, Letlapa decided to marry his girlfriend, who was expecting their second child.

Life, Letlapa thought, is like smooth and attractive sea waters—seemingly innocent but concealing hidden animals and creatures. Similarly, people on Earth may appear innocent, but their actions can be bad and dangerous. They may dislike what you like and seek to destroy the good things you do. Yet, in times of need, they may provide assistance, only to mock you when you're down and out.

Letlapa's marriage faced its fair share of challenges, like any other. Yet, their commitment and determination proved unyielding through thick and thin. Things took a turn when their third child came into the world.

# CHAPTER 2

Letlapa toiled diligently, ensuring a secure home for his family. His daughters excelled in school, earning prestigious honors degrees from top universities. Meanwhile, his wife embarked on a spiritual journey, first becoming a Church Minister and later rising to the esteemed position of Bishop. Adding to her accomplishments, she received an Honorary Doctorate in theology from a Holy Nation Bible College.

Letlapa continued working steadfastly until he reached the age of retirement, having built a life of resilience, accomplishments, and enduring love.

# CHAPTER 3

## EXPULSION, 1976 UPRISING AND UNEMPLOYMENT

A fruit tree you plant does not guarantee delicious fruits.

The life of Letlapa post-high school was rocky and unfortunate.

Letlapa breezed through Grade 12, scoring well. He secured a scholarship from the Lion Match Company to pursue a Junior Secondary Teacher's Course at Setotolwane Teachers Training College. Packing his belongings into a sturdy steel trunk, Letlapa hopped on a train bound for Polokwane, where he was warmly received and provided accommodation.

# CHAPTER 3

During this period, winds of change swept through the country. On one side, there was a whispering breeze, while on the other, the National Party Government stood firm against student protests and opposition parties operating beyond South Africa's borders. The primary source of discontent among students was the forced adoption of Afrikaans as the language of instruction. The community, too, grappled with immoral and unjust practices imposed upon them.

However, Letlapa's journey took an unexpected turn. Just two months into his college adventure, he found himself expelled. He was accused of being one of the instigators from the township, aiming to disrupt the tranquil atmosphere at Setotolwane College.

His dear old mom felt a heavy heart when he walked through the door, sharing the tough news of his expulsion. Even though Letlapa getting kicked out of Teacher Training College, where he was learning to be a teacher, was a real downer, little did they know it was like a tricky blessing in disguise.

**The desired dream was shattered- However his spirit was rejuvenated. Impossible became I'am possible.**

The second lesson he shared was about joining the South African Police (SAP). However, he decided against it because being a police officer meant being seen as an adversary due to enforcing the policies of the National Party Government.

He believed that one learns more from failure than success. Failures point out the mistakes, allowing for corrections and eventual success. Failure, he thought, is the ultimate remedy

# EXPULSION, 1976 UPRISING AND UNEMPLOYMENT

for achieving success.

His parents instilled in him a strong sense of morals, teaching him about standards of behavior and the principles of right and wrong. This upbringing guided him away from joining a gang or engaging in activities that could have led to jail time. Instead, it reinforced his commitment to pursuing his goals and becoming what he aspired to be in the future.

Becoming who you aspire to be is no easy feat but it is possible. He emphasized that recognizing your morals is a crucial first step in this journey.

Moreover, he harnessed the might of the subconscious mind, echoing Goodman's notion that although humans are born to thrive, societal conditioning often leads them astray. Leveraging the subconscious mind's power, one can defy the odds and shape their desired destiny.

Letlapa crafted a personalized, practical blueprint for success. This plan embraced SMART goals — Specific, Measurable, Attainable, Realistic, and Time-bound.

Central to the plan was the need for a robust foundation, and Letlapa identified education as the cornerstone. However, he challenged the conventional belief that education alone unlocks the door to success.

Instead, he likened education to a sunscreen, a shield against the sun's harmful UV rays. While education opens the door, the true challenges and opportunities lie beyond, shrouded in

# CHAPTER 3

uncertainty until one musters the courage to step through.

In Letlapa's perspective, education serves as a protective layer, shielding individuals from the harsh realities that might intimidate them once they venture beyond the familiar threshold. Just as sunscreen guards against sun damage, education provides a safeguard against the unseen obstacles on the path to success.

Sunscreen is like your shield against the sun's mood swings. Imagine the sun as your boss, and sunscreen as your secret weapon. It gives you a sturdy base to face challenges and tackle your work enemies head-on.

Back in the day, HF Verwoerd, part of the National Party Government, came up with Bantu Education. It aimed to keep Black folks in check, making them obedient and less brainy. Funny thing is, despite the not-so-great education, many people still managed to snag university degrees.

Letlapa, though, figured out that wanting an education without a plan was like hunting for a needle in the dark. Sometimes, the best things don't come from the best situations. Even the bad stuff can push you to be your best self.

Letlapa found himself jobless for a good three months. It was a rough patch with no cash flowing in. But here's the thing - he didn't drown his sorrows in alcohol. That's a win right there, a victory over frustration.

***One must not be told what to do, but should rather be***

# EXPULSION, 1976 UPRISING AND UNEMPLOYMENT

*grown in what he wants to achieve.*

# CHAPTER 4

## JOURNEY OF SEEKING EMPLOYMENT

**The future rewards those who press on; I do not have time to feel sorry for myself. I do not have time to complain. I am going to press on (Barrack Obama).**

Every journey comes with its own set of challenges. You either reach your destination safely or not at all. Having a positive mindset is crucial to achieving your goals. Desperation should be banished from your thoughts.

Finding a job was no easy task, especially without knowing someone on the inside. People had to visit companies, asking the security officials at the gate if there were any job openings.

# JOURNEY OF SEEKING EMPLOYMENT

Job agencies seemed to cater only to Whites and Coloured individuals.

In desperate need of employment, he longed for a job to provide for his child and family. A salary was his lifeline, and the hurdles in his way only fueled his determination.

**First Step**

Letlapa got wind of a company that was on the lookout for new hires. Excited, he made his way to the company's entrance, only to find a bustling crowd already gathered.

Suddenly, a stern Personnel Officer, dressed in black, stepped forward and declared, "If you have a Standard 10 Certificate, insert it into your ID document and place them both in this box." Obediently, everyone followed the instructions. The officer collected the box and vanished into a room nearby.

An hour later, he reappeared with the box. To everyone's surprise, he emptied it out and announced, "No jobs available, folks. Collect your documents."

Pandemonium broke loose as people frantically searched for their IDs and certificates. Unfortunately, Letlapa was among those who couldn't locate his Standard 10 Certificate—someone had either intentionally taken it or mistakenly grabbed the wrong one.

It was a gloomy day for Letlapa. Back at home, he shared the unfortunate incident with his friends, reflecting on the unex-

## CHAPTER 4

pected turn of events.

"This is the new South Africa," one friend observed.

"What do you mean?" Letlapa inquired.

"Nothing comes for free. You want a job, you gotta pay. No pay, no job," the friend explained.

"That's terrible! What's the use of going to school?" Letlapa exclaimed.

"To get a piece of paper – a certificate – so you can pay a bribe for a job," the friend replied.

"I went through the same thing last week," another friend added.

"That Personnel Officer, when he said insert your Standard 10 Certificate in your ID, he meant slip a R10 note in there," chimed in another friend.

"That guy must be crazy! Who expects a job seeker to have money?" Letlapa exclaimed.

"He should be reported," Letlapa continued, shaking his head.

"But if you report him, you'll be blacklisted. Most of those Personnel Officers are buddies, and they all pull the same

# JOURNEY OF SEEKING EMPLOYMENT

stunt," warned another friend. "Just let bygones be bygones."

Letlapa felt tension and depression creeping in. His dream of landing a job seemed to be slipping away. Despite the discouragement, he reminded himself that giving up wouldn't solve anything; he had to take action to secure a job.

While some resorted to illegal activities for quick cash, Letlapa decided against it. He knew there had to be a better way.

**Second Step**

One day, Letlapa went to visit his sister and met Sam, the brother of his sister's husband. As they chatted, Sam inquired about Letlapa's employment status. Letlapa shared that he was currently unemployed and recounted a challenging incident involving R10 and a Standard 10 Certificate.

"It's tough these days to secure a job without any connections," Sam remarked. "Tomorrow, at around 7:00 AM, come to Noristan Laboratories, where I work. I'll speak to the Personnel Officer and try to arrange a job for you. When you arrive at the Reception, ask the Receptionist to call me. Make sure to dress formally," Sam advised Letlapa.

True to his word, the next day, Letlapa arrived at Noristan Laboratories promptly at 7:00 AM. He approached the Reception and informed the Receptionist that he was there to meet Sam. After a short wait, Sam appeared in the Reception Area.

Sam led Letlapa to a specific office, where a white man sat

## CHAPTER 4

behind a desk.

"Good morning, Sir," greeted Sam to the white man.

"Morning, Sam. What can I do for you?" the white man inquired.

"This is my son I mentioned. He finished Standard 10 and urgently needs a job to support his child," explained Sam.

"Alright, I understand. But I need to check if we have any vacancies," replied the white man, introducing himself as Mr. Van Tonder.

"What's your name?" Van Tonder asked Letlapa.

"Letlapa."

"Okay, wait for me at the reception; I'll come back to you," Van Tonder instructed.

After about an hour, Sam returned to the reception and brought Letlapa back to Van Tonder's office.

"This guy is very clever; you won't regret giving him a job," Sam assured Van Tonder.

"You're in luck; there's a job in the Laboratory for an Assistant Laboratory Technician," Van Tonder announced.

# JOURNEY OF SEEKING EMPLOYMENT

Van Tonder had a condition before giving Letlapa the job—he insisted on an aptitude test. If Letlapa performed well, the job was his. Letlapa took the test, aced it after two hours, and secured the position.

However, there was a snag. Van Tonder noticed that Letlapa's Standard 10 Certificate lacked Mathematics and Science, crucial for a Laboratory Technician role.

"Letlapa, your certificate doesn't have Math and Science. Those are essential for this job," Van Tonder pointed out.

Letlapa, quick on his feet, fibbed, "Yes, Sir, but I learned them in Form 3 due to a lack of teachers in Standard 10."

Concerned, Van Tonder asked, "How do you plan to fix this?"

"I'll study them at night school," Letlapa promptly replied.

Accepting the plan, Van Tonder said, "Alright, you're on twelve months' probation. Once you pass those subjects, we'll review your status."

Letlapa diligently attended night school, aced the subjects, and had his probation confirmed, securing his position.

Noristan Laboratories, a German company making medicines and studying traditional remedies, had David on board. His role involved assessing the raw materials for pharmaceuticals, and the process included weighing them on a scale.

## CHAPTER 4

One day, David was paired up with Letlapa to assist with the tasks. However, David didn't warm up to Letlapa, fearing he might lose his job. Despite this, David took on the responsibility of teaching Letlapa how to use the weigh-scale balance.

In a somewhat crude attempt at humor, David teased Letlapa, "Handle the buttons on this scale as delicately as you would touch your wife's thighs." Letlapa remained silent, choosing not to respond.

Growing frustrated, David prodded Letlapa further, "I'm talking to you. Can't you hear?" Letlapa replied, "No." Annoyed, David retorted, "Then answer when I ask you something!"

Over the next three months, Letlapa learned the ropes and became proficient at the job. He no longer needed David's supervision, marking the end of their working relationship.

The company rolled out an In-house Training program. Letlapa, eager to learn, completed all the modules within a year and was swiftly promoted to a full-fledged Laboratory Technician.

Just five months into the job, chaos struck during the June 1976 Riots. As the clock approached 4:00 PM, time to head home, Mr. Van Tonder, the Personnel Officer, entered the Laboratory with a grave warning. He urged them to stay at work due to the unrest in Mamelodi, cautioning that they might face harm from the rioting students.

# JOURNEY OF SEEKING EMPLOYMENT

This news didn't sit well with Letlapa and the others, as their loved ones were in Mamelodi. Disregarding the advice, they shed their white coats and made their way home. The journey from Noristan Laboratories to Mamelodi was a challenging 10 km walk.

Entering Mamelodi from the west, they encountered a traffic circle surrounded by shops, including a Municipal Bottle Store. The air was thick with smoke from municipal buildings set ablaze, and the scene was chaotic with people looting the bottle stores. Even the once vibrant Mamelodi Library, where Letlapa and others had learned Life Skills, was engulfed in flames and sadly, it was never rebuilt.

In those days, there were no worker unions, and the Congress of South African Trade Unions (COSATU) was just starting to take shape. The political atmosphere was thick with tension. South African Defense vehicles moved slowly through the township, and a curfew was enforced.

From 7:00 PM onwards, people were not allowed to wander the streets. Soldiers were on the lookout for those they called "klip gooiers" or stone throwers—individuals opposing the government. Anyone found outside was arrested, and many disappeared, some never to be found again.

Political activists were fleeing the country, seeking exile. Some came back after 1994, while others remained absent. Then, a new group known as "Comrades" emerged. These individuals were fierce. Those suspected of collaborating with the police faced brutal beatings or even death. The township was filled with political tension, and trust among residents was scarce.

# CHAPTER 4

Various political strategies were employed to destabilize the National Party Government, such as the Rent boycott. Houses belonging to certain police members were targeted with petrol bombs. The situation was dire, and survival meant pretending to agree with the Comrades, even if your beliefs differed.

Decades ago, a group of friends, known as the Comrades, dedicated themselves to improving their township. They worked hard to clean up the area and significantly reduce crime. In 1978, one of them, Letlapa, married his high school sweetheart, who was expecting their second child.

Letlapa, determined to provide a stable home for his growing family, secured a 99-year lease for a piece of land and built a spacious four-room house. At that time, he already had three daughters, with the youngest yet to be born when they moved into their new home.

This marked the beginning of a new chapter in Letlapa's life at his parents' house. However, around 1982, Mamelodi faced a call from political organizations urging the community to boycott rent payments. On November 21, 1985, the community peacefully protested, aiming to deliver a memorandum to Mayor Bennet Ndlazi, opposing rent and service charges.

Tragically, what started as a peaceful march turned into a catastrophe. The South African Defence Force (SADF) and the South African Police (SAP) opened fire on the protesters, resulting in the heartbreaking loss of 13 lives, including a 13-month-old child named Trocier Ndlovu.

Tension gripped Mamelodi, where suspicions ran high,

# JOURNEY OF SEEKING EMPLOYMENT

branding some as government informants. A brutal method called necklacing, involving placing a car tire around the accused's neck and setting it ablaze, became a terrifying reality.

In this volatile atmosphere, each person viewed the other as an adversary. Mamelodi was divided into sections, each governed by youth groups known as "Comrades." These Comrades had various responsibilities, from maintaining cleanliness to meting out punishment to those accused of theft.

One day, the Comrades descended upon Letlapa's home. Their numbers were many, their voices rising in political struggle songs. Frightened, Letlapa's wife and children sought refuge indoors.

"Good day," the Comrade Leader greeted Letlapa.

"Good day, Comrades," Letlapa responded, tension evident in his voice.

"Don't be afraid; we're not here to harm you. We come in peace," assured the Leader.

They entered the yard, and amidst chants, they engaged Letlapa in conversation about the ongoing struggle and political matters. Eventually, the Leader spoke, "Comrade, we've come to elect you as our Community Leader."

In response, Letlapa expressed gratitude for the offer but explained his inability. He cited a speech impediment that caused him to stammer, making leadership challenging for him.

## CHAPTER 4

"Hey there, Comrade! We've been chatting for nearly an hour, and you haven't stumbled or shown any trouble with your speech," The Leader observed.

"Are you turning us down because you're in cahoots with the Police?" they inquired impatiently.

"Nope, not at all," Letlapa replied.

"Alright then, Comrade, what's your decision?" they pressed.

"Okay, I'm cool with it—I accept your request," Letlapa conceded.

"Thank you, Comrade. ***AMANDLA! WETHU.AMANDLA! VIVA OUR LEADER! VIVA***" They sang struggle songs on their way out of the yard.

Letlapa, a guy from the neighborhood, ended up becoming the go-to person in his community. He took on the role of a leader, dealing with issues like accusations of stealing or worse.

His day job was going pretty well too. There was this committee thing that popped up at work to handle complaints from the workers. When it was time to talk about getting paid more, the committee met with the bosses a bunch of times.

Then came the big meeting. The bosses, feeling all bold, said, "Hey, if anyone here thinks our company is some kind of charity, feel free to find a better job." Ouch, right? It hurt a lot. The next year, loads of people, including Letlapa, left the company.

# JOURNEY OF SEEKING EMPLOYMENT

Those employees resigned to join other companies.

***The future rewards those who press on; I do not have time to feel sorry for myself. I do not have time to complain. I am going to press on*** (Barrack Obama)

**Third Step**

In 1983, Letlapa made a big change in his career. He said goodbye to his old job and joined a new company called SC Johnson Wax. Every day, he hopped on a bus to get to work. His role at the company was pretty cool – he was a Laboratory Technician.

At SC Johnson Wax, they were busy making things that people use every day. They made furniture polish, auto care polishes, air sanitizers, floor polishes, and even toilet care products. These were not just for homes, but also for businesses and factories. In the Laboratory where Letlapa worked, there were three other technicians, and he became the fourth member of the team.

After working hard for three years, Letlapa got a big promotion – he became a Supervisor. But, guess what? His co-workers, who had been part of the company for a long time, didn't exactly throw a party to celebrate his promotion. They weren't too happy about it.

**Obstacles don't have to stop you. If you run into a wall, don't turn around and give up. Figure out how to climb it, go through it, or work around it:** ( Michel Jordan).

## CHAPTER 4

A workplace is like a gathering of diverse minds, each vying in their own way. In every workplace, you'll find both essential and avoidable relationship hiccups:

Among coworkers,

Between an employee and a manager, or

Among managers.

Nothing ominous there. The real challenge lies in the avoidable tiffs.

The official attire consisted of a white coat and safety glasses. Commuting from Mamelodi Township to Rosslyn, he'd get off the bus around 200 meters from the factory.

One rainy day, he arrived at the factory soaked through. Having to change into dry clothes, he switched to overalls and safety shoes before resuming his daily tasks.

After he shook the raindrops off, he changed into his dry clothes, only to realize his shoes weren't where he'd left them to dry. Puzzled, he asked his colleagues in the lab, but each one denied knowing their whereabouts.

In his quest, he stumbled upon his shoes beneath a hidden table, a casualty of the intense heat. The lab cleaner disclosed that his colleagues had tossed them into a microwave to speed up the drying process before stashing them away.

"How could you do such a mischievous thing?" Letlapa confronted them.

Silence followed. They merely chuckled and departed for home, leaving Letlapa with a heavy heart. He went home, wearing a pair of safety shoes.

Once there, he recounted the incident to his family.

"Shouldn't you report them?" his wife inquired.

"No," Letlapa replied.

"Why not? This is serious. Next time, they might even harm you," his wife cautioned.

"It's tricky. I didn't witness them putting the shoes in the microwave," Letlapa explained.

"But did the cleaner really tell you?" The Wife inquired.

"Yes, she did," Letlapa confirmed. "But you know, that's just hearsay," he added.

Letlapa then shared his perspective, "Sometimes, dealing with an enemy is like guiding a toddler. Hold their hand, teach them to walk, and they might start liking you."

"It's your decision," the Wife remarked.

# CHAPTER 4

Deep in thought, Letlapa pondered several questions:

Is his wife right? Should he report them?

How can he prevent such animalistic behavior in the future?

Could this be a sign that his colleagues don't like him?

Recognizing the potential consequences of such incidents—fights, resignations, animosity, and more—Letlapa weighed his options. Eventually, he decided against reporting them. Instead, he chose not to retaliate or resign. After all, that company belonged to none of them; they were all just workers trying to earn a living for their families.

The next day, Letlapa considered telling his boss about the incident but hesitated. He hadn't witnessed the wrongdoing himself; it was just gossip, and he didn't want to strain his relationship with the cleaner and others.

"Why? It's a serious matter. They might harm you next time," his wife cautioned. "But it's your decision."

Letlapa pondered:

Is his wife right about reporting them?

How can he prevent such behavior in the future?

Does this suggest his colleagues harbor ill feelings toward

him?

Ultimately, Letlapa decided not to harbor hatred for his colleagues. Instead, he blamed himself for entertaining their harmful actions. He pledged to rise above it and continue with his life as if nothing happened.

The next morning, Letlapa greeted his colleagues and bid them farewell in the afternoon when he left for home. Whether they responded or not didn't concern him.

What his colleagues did to him felt like unfair treatment, driven by discrimination and jealousy simply because they couldn't comprehend why he became their supervisor.

His education, knowledge, and skills helped him stand strong against their negative actions. Seeking to understand them better, he spent weekends visiting their homes and attending events like funerals. However, Letlapa's efforts were met with resistance from one colleague's wife, who disliked his presence at such occasions.

Letlapa's motivation to bridge gaps and diffuse tension stemmed from a sermon he heard at church, based on Isaiah 41:10 - "So do not fear, for I am with you, do not be dismayed, for I am your God. I will strengthen you and help you, I will uphold you with my righteous right hand." This message inspired him to approach challenges with courage.

The guidance continued with a lesson from Psalm 37:4-5 - "Take delight in the Lord, and He will give you the desires of

# CHAPTER 4

your heart." Letlapa embraced this teaching, finding strength in his faith and the belief that his positive actions would ultimately prevail.

These two little verses transformed his life, mindset, and character. He started embracing others more warmly, even cherishing those who opposed him because their animosity fueled his success.

Letlapa turned into a more assertive person, crafting a tiny book filled with these verses and uplifting quotes. He carried it everywhere, reading it:

On the bus to and from home and work,

At home, lounging in front of the TV,

Before bedtime,

During breakfast before heading to work, and

During lunch breaks.

The results were astonishing. He snagged the role of the first black Personnel and Safety Officer, answering to the Personnel Manager Chairperson of the Liaison Committee. He became a part of the Junior Management Committee and a member of the Job Evaluation Committee.

To ensure his unconventional role bore fruit, Letlapa was dispatched to Egypt to grasp more about rendering Trade Unions

# JOURNEY OF SEEKING EMPLOYMENT

unnecessary. Simultaneously, other Personnel Officers underwent training in various subsidiary companies.

The training aimed to give Personal Officers the tools to persuade colleagues against joining Trade Unions upon returning to their respective companies. The company's management regularly reminded employees that the owner, somewhere in the United States, preferred a union-free workforce. Joining a union risked losing perks like profit-sharing bonuses and non-interest home loans, benefits the employees had grown accustomed to.

Despite increasing bond rates, an unemployed wife, and children attending school, the salary was no longer enough. In response, Letlapa took on a part-time role as an insurance seller after his regular work hours. Selling insurance policies brought in extra income, providing financial relief until his wife found employment.

The key to achieving success lies in the determination to face failures and find solutions. Letlapa's perseverance paid off, and he was recognized with "The Housing Employee of the Year Award" for his efforts in helping fellow employees acquire homes and become homeowners.

**If we don't change, we don't grow. If we don't grow, we aren't living** (Gail Sheehy).

**Fourth Step And Last Step**

Fifteen years at SC Johnson Wax, and Letlapa was ready for

## CHAPTER 4

a change. He left his job and joined the National Government Department as a Specialist in Employment Relations Management (formerly known as Labour Relations).

But a year or two later, his former colleagues at SC Johnson Wax faced dismissal. Some reached out to Letlapa for help in finding new jobs in the Government.

Life, like a Festival of Minds, brings both protagonists and antagonists. If not handled carefully, the latter can cast a shadow of fear, making someone afraid of their own actions. This fear can prevent a person from overcoming the challenges posed by antagonists and achieving success in life. It's the fear that holds them back from taking the necessary steps.

***Manage a negative environment to avoid becoming negatively charged.***

In the tightly controlled world of government institutions, Letlapa found himself in a challenging probation period lasting twelve months. During this time, he navigated the complex landscape of Public Service with little guidance, left to either swim or sink.

Despite the lack of a formal introduction to the workings of Public Service, Letlapa received a warm welcome, particularly from his supportive White Female Supervisor. His role as Assistant Director: Labour Relations (Middle Management) came with the responsibility of overseeing a sub-directorate, comprising himself and a subordinate with extensive experience in public service.

# JOURNEY OF SEEKING EMPLOYMENT

Tasked with transforming the Labour Relations Sub-directorate into a fully functional unit, Letlapa faced the daunting task of addressing numerous grievances and misconduct cases. The department, home to two major unions, relied on the internal Departmental Bargaining Council as a platform for discussions between department representatives and unions, where employer policy documents were adopted.

As the head of the Labour Relations unit, Letlapa assumed the crucial role of being the department's spokesperson in these meetings. However, the absence of established Labour Relations Policies and Guidelines contributed to a growing number of grievances and misconduct cases. Determined to make a positive impact, Letlapa dedicated time to formulate comprehensive Labour Relations Policies to address the issues at hand.

Letlapa had a crucial role—handling employee grievances and misconduct cases in the Department. Many folks were quitting to get their pension money early, but soon, their funds ran out. Letlapa dug into the issue and found out they didn't know the ins and outs of early pension withdrawals.

To help them out, Letlapa started a Pre-Retirement Programme. It aimed to educate employees planning to retire in 5, 10, and 15 years, as well as those just curious about pensions. The Public Service, where Letlapa now worked, had strict rules compared to his previous job in the private sector.

In the private sector, not everything needed a report, and reaching out to management wasn't a big deal—quite different from the public service's regulated environment.

# CHAPTER 4

Juniors don't usually go to the Director General (DG) unless it's really necessary or they've been summoned. The other day, Letlapa needed the DG's signature to approve his request to visit a Regional Office for a disciplinary hearing the next day. Since his supervisor wasn't around, Letlapa headed to the DG's office.

To Letlapa's surprise, the DG was taken aback to see him there. The DG questioned Letlapa about who he was, where his supervisor was, and advised him to follow the proper protocol instead of just entering the office for a signature. This caught Letlapa off guard because, in the Private Sector, it's not uncommon to approach a manager's office, especially for urgent matters.

The next day, the supervisor was back at work and called Letlapa to address the situation, reprimanding him for his actions.

"Is there a problem?" Letlapa asked.

"Yes," the supervisor replied.

"Why?" Letlapa inquired.

"In the world of public service, there's a dance, a rhythm to follow. You can't just waltz into the offices of the Director, Chief Director, Deputy Director-General, or Director-General without a nod from yours truly," the Supervisor emphasized.

"Well, I get it now. The private sector doesn't bother with these public service formalities," Letlape remarked.

# JOURNEY OF SEEKING EMPLOYMENT

With a diplomatic nod, the Supervisor ushered Letlape to meet the DG, explaining that the new guy wasn't well-versed in the intricacies of public service protocols. The DG extended a warm welcome, marking the commencement of a newfound alliance.

However, not all line Managers were keen on introducing their subordinates. This task fell on Letlape's shoulders, earning him more than a few unkind nicknames. Colleagues labeled him as "10111" (SAPS Emergency telephone number), the "Hanging Judge," and the "Scorpion."

Adding insult to injury, many employees began to fear Letlape. Every conversation he had with someone triggered a wave of speculation. If he visited a Regional Office, the atmosphere turned uneasy as employees anticipated trouble in the air.

The Internship Programme opened doors for interns to gain work experience. After it ended, some secured positions, but Letlapa found himself stuck in lower roles, despite others rising to Director positions. Frustrated, he couldn't quit due to six more years until his pension at sixty-five.

During this time, Letlapa achieved a remarkable feat: winning the "Employee of the Year Award." His reward included a handsome cash prize and a family trip to Cape Town, covering everything from accommodation to a rented vehicle. Exploring Cape Town, they visited iconic spots like Robben Island, Cape Point, and the Castle.

When the Director role was advertised, Letlapa hesitated to apply. He felt skeptical, fearing political interference might

# CHAPTER 4

hinder his chances, despite his remarkable achievements.

But then, his gut feeling told him to give it a shot. So, he did. He applied, got shortlisted, and faced a series of interviews. The climax? A three-day psychological test.

Guess what? He nailed it. He snagged the role of a Director – a Senior Manager, to be precise.

Things took a twist when he earned an award for efficiently handling misconduct cases in the Public Service. The Department of Performance, Monitoring, and Evaluation oversaw this process. Here's the kicker: not everyone was cheering. Many managers weren't thrilled about it. Why? Because they wanted to boot out employees who weren't playing by the rules of the Disciplinary Code and Procedures.

And thus began a real tug of war. On one side, the unions voiced concerns about cozying up to management. On the flip side, management griped about shielding employees.

Work turned sour. Going to the office became a chore. There were more foes than friends among the colleagues.

Letlapa led numerous workshops focusing on the reasons behind misconduct, guiding employees through the process of disciplinary hearings, and illustrating how they could raise grievances. Participants delved into understanding the distinctions between Grievance of Right and Grievance of Interest. The latter involves a complaint about something of personal interest, unsupported by legislation but desired by the employee.

In instances where an employee raised a grievance of interest and it remained unresolved to their satisfaction, blame often fell on Letlapa's unit, accused of siding with management. Undeterred by negativity, Letlapa maintained a positive outlook and refrained from engaging with those who pointed fingers at him. He emphasized that strength doesn't guarantee perpetual dominance; even the mighty can become powerless over time.

Letlapa viewed the workplace as a celebration of diverse minds competing for the betterment of overall institutional performance, steering away from fostering enmity among participants.

***No matter the dire situation always laugh like a Hyena otherwise you will laugh forever like a fleshless human being.***

CHAPTER: 5

# CHAPTER 5

## LATER YEARS

The bird's-eye view of the forest is stunning, but hidden dangers lurk within. Anyone strolling through might face unexpected hurdles—known and unknown species, a variety of animals, mysterious paths, ever-changing weather, and a medley of trees, each with the potential to bring peril.

This woodland is home to creatures that could harm a person, either by causing injury or worse. Venomous insects might deliver painful bites, leading to cuts, swelling, or changes in skin color. There's also the risk of getting lost, vanishing without a trace, or falling prey to thieves concealed among the trees.

# LATER YEARS

Surviving in this environment demands not only physical strength but also mental sharpness. Perseverance, commitment, and unwavering focus are crucial. Without these qualities, facing the challenges of the forest becomes not just difficult but nearly impossible.

The time for careful consideration and examining every potential danger along Letlapa's path has come to an end.

He dashed through his journey, ticking off his personal milestones. No more hurdles stood in his way.

As the sun dipped below the horizon, it signaled the moment to hang up his work hat and explore activities once elusive during his nine-to-five grind. The wisdom, abilities, and inner strength honed over his years of employment became a formidable arsenal, mightier than the united forces of the world.

In retirement, he lent a helping hand to countless souls within the church, local communities, and among friends. His knack for problem-solving became a beacon, guiding others through their challenges.

***Yamada aptly remarked, "Let's nudge people to scrutinize problems closely, unveiling the hidden possibilities they may cradle."***

# Part Three

# CHAPTER 6

## MARIA AND SELEPE

In the town of Kilnerton, there lived a man named Peter Serumula and his wife Selina. Together, they created a family of four, including their two children, Maria and Selepe. The Serumula family was known as the Parrot Family, always focusing on the positive aspects of life, often indulging in lavish gifts at gatherings and in their church community.

Peter, a Manager at a Local Government Institution, wore another hat as an Evangelist in his church. Selina, on the other hand, was a skilled Nurse working at a local clinic. Their lives seemed picture-perfect, but there was a twist in the tale.

While the Serumula parents were busy enjoying the brighter

## CHAPTER 6

side of life, their children, Maria and Selepe, were left to their own devices. The parents, in their generosity, neglected instilling a sense of responsibility and independence in their kids.

Trouble began to brew when Selepe, the younger of the two, dropped out of school and fell into the clutches of township gangsterism, gaining a notorious reputation. Maria, the elder sibling, enjoyed her time at school but found herself entangled with a boyfriend at an early age.

Despite Maria's charm, vivacity, and academic success, her notorious brother, Selepe, fiercely protected her. It was as if he guarded her like someone shielding a delicious cup of coffee from a pesky fly. Many boys were intimidated and hesitant to approach Maria, fearing the wrath of Selepe.

And so, the Parrot Family, with all its extravagance, faced the consequences of neglecting the guidance their children truly needed. The tale of Peter, Selina, Maria, and Selepe unfolded with unexpected twists and turns, teaching a lesson about the delicate balance between indulgence and responsibility in the journey of life.

However, Kolobe wasn't scared of Selepe. He and Maria had started dating, and their favorite hangout spots included Jazz Festivals at HM Pitjie Stadium in Mamelodi. Occasionally, they'd visit shebeens to enjoy some music. While Maria abstained from alcohol, her friends were casual drinkers.

Word got to Selepe through his grapevine that his younger sister, Maria, was spending time with a particular boy. This news ignited his anger, and he set out to find this young man.

One day, as Maria, Kolobe, and their friends were chilling at a local park, Selepe suddenly appeared and confronted Kolobe.

"Are you the guy dating my sister?" Selepe asked angrily, pointing a finger at Kolobe.

Kolobe, unfazed, replied, "What kind of question is that?"

"Don't be disrespectful, young man. I asked a question, and I expect an answer," Selepe retorted in frustration.

Smirking, Kolobe suggested, "Why not ask your sister?"

Turning to Maria, Selepe questioned, "Is he your boyfriend?"

Maria confidently replied, "Yes."

Breathing heavily, Selepe commanded, "Stand up and go home. I don't ever want to see you with this boy again. Do you understand?"

I'm going my own way. You can't decide how I live," Maria shot back defiantly.

Selepe, angered by her response, lunged at Kolobe. Security personnel intervened upon witnessing Selepe's attack, promptly instructing him to leave the stadium.

## CHAPTER 6

Back home, Maria confided in her mother about Selepe's actions. Her mother assured her that she would address the situation.

Undeterred, Kolobe and Maria continued their outings – be it to parties, picnics, or simply window-shopping in town. The township hosted trendy weekend parties, organized by locals with names inspired by famous American musical groups like the Commodores and the Spinners.

These gatherings were a haven for music and romance enthusiasts. Vinyl records spun on record players provided the soundtrack, as attendees sipped on alcoholic beverages, swaying alone or with their significant others. The festivities often stretched into the early hours of the next day.

Unbeknownst to their parents, Sello and Kolobe frequented parties together. One day, as they strolled home from school, Sello urged Kolobe to end his relationship with Maria due to her brother's dangerous reputation.

"Sello, Selepe is crazy. I won't break up with Maria," Kolobe firmly replied.

"I'm just looking out for you. That guy is trouble," Sello warned.

"Who does he think he is, telling me to break up with someone I love? Is he planning to marry her himself?" Kolobe questioned.

"The choice is yours," Sello replied.

"Oh, by the way, tomorrow's Saturday. Want to hit up the Spinners Party to take a break from studying?" Kolobe invited.

"Absolutely! Let's bring Tau and Mollo," Sello agreed.

"Bringing your girlfriend?" Kolobe inquired.

"Nah, I don't want to make a habit of partying with her," Sello explained.

"Alright, cool," Kolobe nodded.

"Eish! No money for drinks," sighed Sello.

"I've got it covered," replied Kolobe.

They went their separate ways, heading home. The next day, Saturday, found them at the Spinners Party. In no time, Maria joined them. As always, Letlapa, Sello, and Tau stuck together, sitting at a table, chatting about life post-grade 12.

Kolobe and Maria, caught in the rhythm, got up to dance. Curious onlookers watched them, seemingly amazed by the sight of a good-looking girl dancing with someone like Kolobe.

Enter Selepe, either intoxicated or sober—his walk made it hard to tell. Spotting his sister Maria dancing with Kolobe, he charged towards them.

## CHAPTER 6

"I've warned you to stay away from my sister, and you just won't listen. From now on, I don't want to see you two together, got it?" Selepe angrily told Kolobe.

In the midst of a lively gathering, Kolobe, slightly out of breath, declared to Selepe, "This is my girlfriend, and I won't end things with her. We're in love."

Selepe, raising his voice, retorted, "Listen, young man, she's my younger sister. She's not ready for love. Break up with her."

Selepe's booming voice disrupted the party, grabbing everyone's attention. The dancing and chatter ceased as all eyes turned to him.

Maria, angered by her brother's interference, shouted, "He's my boyfriend, and I won't break up with him!"

In a fit of rage, Selepe threatened, "Fine, I'll show you a journey to hell you'll look forward to." He brandished a knife and moved menacingly toward Kolobe.

Chaos erupted in the room. Sello, Mollo, and Tau hurried to Kolobe's aid, while Maria desperately called for help, her voice piercing through the commotion.

Selepe's knife dug into Kolobe's thigh, causing a surge of pain. In retaliation, Maria, fueled by anger, swung an empty beer bottle at her brother's head. Reacting swiftly, Sello, Mollo, and Tau intervened, disarming Selepe and rushing the injured Kolobe to a nearby doctor. Luckily, the wound turned out to be less severe than feared.

The incident remained a secret between Selepe, Maria, and the trio who helped Kolobe. However, Maria couldn't keep the truth hidden from her parents. When she finally confessed, her parents were furious and scolded her.

To add to Maria's woes, her parents insisted she end her relationship with Kolobe, asserting that she wasn't ready for the complexities of love. Defiantly, Maria refused to part ways with Kolobe. In response, her father, overwhelmed with frustration, slapped her across the face. Tears streaming down her cheeks, Maria fled the house, caught in the tumult of emotions and family discord.

**The Secret**

The mother, feeling uneasy, was troubled by the fact that Maria and Kolobe shared the same father. Maria's father was also Kolobe's father. She had been involved with him as a concubine while her husband was away on a two-year overseas educational trip. Unfortunately, during the year her husband returned, she discovered she was pregnant.

Upon learning about the pregnancy, she initially wanted to undergo an abortion, but doctors advised against it due to her age and the stage of the fetus's development. Her husband only returned home once a year, and during that time, she fulfilled her marital duties with him. However, about four to six months before his permanent return, she found out about her pregnancy.

# CHAPTER 6

In her husband's absence, she had a romantic relationship with James nearly every week. There was little doubt that James was the father of the unborn Maria. This hidden truth had been weighing on her for a long time, and now it seemed to be resurfacing, causing her inner turmoil.

Will she ever confess to her husband? Or perhaps to Maria? How would they react to her unfaithful behavior? What about her friends and neighbors who hold her in high regard?

James knew that Maria was his daughter, born within his marriage to Selina. Biologically, Kolobe and Maria are half-siblings. Unbeknownst to them, one of their parents engaged in an adulterous affair. The tension between Selepe and Kolobe, seemingly fueled by the unknown connection between Kolobe and Maria, began to trouble Selina. Yet, she hesitated to confront Selepe about it.

Things took a dramatic turn when Maria, unable to bear the situation, slapped Selepe and left home for a week, seeking refuge with her divorced aunt nearby. Kolobe frequently visited her at the aunt's house, and even the aunt remained oblivious to the fact that Kolobe and Maria were half-siblings.

Kolobe, fueled by a desire for revenge against Selepe, confided in his friends about his intentions. Despite their pleas to avoid confrontation, he chose to defy their advice. In a bold move, Kolobe and his friends attended the Spinners Party, where Selepe was present (though Maria was not in attendance). The stage was set for a potentially explosive situation.

Selepe, filled with pride, narrated to his friends how he taught

# MARIA AND SELEPE

Kolobe a lesson by stabbing him in the thigh for refusing to end his relationship with Selepe's sister. As Selepe bragged about his actions, Kolobe overheard the conversation, and his anger reached its peak. He immediately confronted Selepe.

"Hey, barie (foolish person in township language), come here!" Kolobe shouted at Selepe.

"Are you talking to me, boy?" Selepe retorted.

"Yes, you are the only barie in this room," Kolobe responded.

Selepe, now enraged, drew a knife and advanced towards Kolobe. Kolobe quickly exited the room, and Selepe, breathing heavily, followed him outside. Sello, Mollo, and Tau also followed Selepe.

Once outside, Kolobe asserted that Selepe had no authority to dictate his relationship with Maria, and he had no intention of breaking up with her. To emphasize his point, Kolobe humorously declared that he would only part ways with Maria on the day a dog and a pig went to a church to seek the blessings of a minister for their marriage.

Selepe, like a wounded buffalo, couldn't contain his anger and swiftly slapped Kolobe with the speed of lightning.

Kolobe retaliated with a burst of strong punches, and Selepe tumbled to the ground, blood seeping from his mouth. In an instant, Sello, Mollo, and Tau intervened, abruptly ending the brawl. They hastily fled the scene just as onlookers emerged,

# CHAPTER 6

drawn by the commotion.

Although Selepe sustained minor injuries, he chose not to involve the police, opting to inform his parents about the clash with Kolobe. Advised by his parents to avoid direct confrontations, they promised to address the issue with Maria.

Word reached Maria through her friend Pretty during their town encounter. Learning that Kolobe had stood up to Selepe, Maria breathed a sigh of relief, considering it a lesson well-taught.

However, Selepe harbored deep resentment for Kolobe's actions. To compound matters, his friends no longer cowered in fear of him. During a visit to the Spinners Club, he overheard patrons gossiping about him. In a fit of rage, he confronted them with a knife, but fortunately, they managed to escape unscathed.

The Spinners Club got really worried and called the police. They were afraid that things might get worse and that people wouldn't want to come to the club anymore.

When the police showed up, they talked to everyone and then decided to take him away. They told his parents about it too.

After a couple of days, he had to go to the local court. His parents and some family members were there, but Maria wasn't. The court thing didn't take long. Even though he said he didn't do it, the court said he was guilty of having a knife and scaring people.

Then the court asked him to say why he shouldn't get in too much trouble. But he didn't really say much, just looked down and seemed unsure.

The judge told him, "If you don't want to talk, that's like saying you don't care what happens." The judge also said, "Think about all the people who used to be scared of you, and maybe still are. You're probably scared too, more than you've ever been in your life."

You got lucky this time; the knife you made didn't hurt anyone. But I'm giving you six months in jail, hoping you'll learn your lesson. Court's done." The Magistrate stood up and left.

The Police Officer led him away to begin his time behind bars.

# CHAPTER 7

## BROTHEL

**Maria Meets Pretty**

During the recent school break, students were blessed with a break from the usual school grind. With minimal homework on their plates, they had the golden opportunity to savor their free time. Many chose to explore the town, indulge in some window shopping, or catch up with friends and family.

On a particularly sunny day, Maria found herself enjoying a leisurely lunch on a restaurant balcony. To her surprise, her long-lost friend Pretty appeared out of the blue. It had been nearly a year since they last met. Maria couldn't contain her joy and stood up, giving Pretty a warm embrace.

"Where on earth have you been hiding?" Maria asked with curiosity.

"Between the cracks of this world," Pretty replied mysteriously.

Intrigued, Maria prodded, "That sounds fascinating. Tell me more about these cracks."

"Not now. But you, my dear, spill the beans. Why do you still look fabulous after all these years? What's your secret?" Pretty inquired.

"Self-care and steering clear of alcohol," Maria revealed.

"A profound secret indeed. Unfortunately, some of us can't resist alcohol because it feels like the only weapon to combat our struggles," Pretty lamented.

"Struggles, you say? Share more; maybe I can be of help," Maria offered sincerely.

"Let's put that aside for now. It's a topic that might bring tears. On a different note, I heard about your brother being in custody for assaulting your boyfriend. Is that true?" Pretty asked with concern.

# CHAPTER 7

Maria nodded solemnly, confirming the truth of the matter.

Pretty couldn't hide her curiosity as she asked, 'So, are you happy that your boyfriend caused trouble with your brother?'

Maria nodded, 'Yes. He's been meddling in my relationship with Kolobe and even convinced my parents to tell me to stop loving him.'

Maria revealed that she had temporarily moved in with her Aunt after her father slapped her for being in a relationship with Kolobe. Despite the ordeal, she expressed her intention to return home soon.

Pretty then shared her own struggles, explaining that the father of her child had disappeared without a trace. This compelled her to leave school and find a job to support her child. Unfortunately, job opportunities were scarce, and for the past two years, she had been unable to secure stable employment, putting the burden on her parents to care for her child.

Upon hearing Pretty's story, a friend hesitated but eventually suggested unconventional ways for her to earn a living. Now, Pretty can make approximately R6000 to R10000 per month.

"That sounds tough," Maria commented. "But you haven't told me what these unconventional means involve.

"It's a hustler's gig," Pretty replied.

Maria raised an eyebrow. "What's that all about?"

# BROTHEL

"In a nutshell, it's like a business, but some see it as shady, like prostitution, which is often seen as illegal," Pretty clarified.

"What? You're kidding. A lovely girl like you resorting to that?" Maria responded, shocked.

Pretty went on to spill the beans about a client who pays double but gets possessive. He doesn't want her with anyone else, but she goes behind his back.

"I asked him why," Pretty continued. The client revealed that his marriage lacked passion. His wife is always tired, wears underwear to bed, and their love is just tolerance.

Pretty added that this man is married with two kids, and his wife is a nurse. Excusing herself, Pretty went to the bathroom. As she pulled out a tissue from her bag, a business card slipped to the floor. Maria grabbed it swiftly and discreetly tucked it into her own bag.

Maria quickly looked at the business card. The card read:

Department of Forestry

James R. Serumula

Project Manager

Tel: 012-898 1234

# CHAPTER 7

Fax: 012-898 2468

Curiosity bubbled within her, a question echoing in her mind like a persistent whisper. Could this be the person she knows? Is this her father? The uncertainty gnawed at her, urging her to find answers. Restlessness consumed her, pushing her to contemplate leaving.

Upon her return from the bathroom, Maria couldn't contain her curiosity and inquired, "Who is this mysterious rich client of yours, Pretty?"

Maintaining confidentiality, Pretty replied, "In our line of work, we don't reveal our clients' identities."

The unanswered questions weighed on Maria, prompting her to stand up and express her intention to leave. Pretty, puzzled, questioned Maria's sudden departure, to which Maria vaguely replied, "It's not a big deal. Let's forget about it."

Maria elaborated, "Besides, knowing affluent individuals might come in handy. You never know when you might need financial assistance, and it's good to know who to turn to."

Accepting Maria's explanation, Pretty bid her farewell, acknowledging the unpredictable nature of the world. Maria echoed the sentiment, saying, "Let it be like that," as she made her exit, leaving the door open for future encounters.

On her way to the taxi, a strange thought whispered to Maria – the rich man might be her father. The notion lingered as she hesitated, clutching the business card in her hand. At home, the curiosity grew, compelling her to retreat to her bedroom.

In the quiet of her aunt's house, Maria settled on the bed and unfolded the business card. Her eyes scanned its details, and with each glance, a realization sank in – this was her father's card. A mix of disbelief and discomfort settled within her. Could her father really be involved with her friend, or more delicately put, a woman in that line of work?

Questions swirled in her mind. Why would her father venture into such a clandestine world, leaving his seemingly happy home behind? Was there trouble between him and Mom? Maria pondered the secrets concealed within their shared bedroom, wondering if her mother was aware of this dual life.

The enigma deepened as Maria grappled with the possibility of her friend Pretty being connected to the rich man who might be her father. Sleep offered no respite, and she awoke only when her aunt returned from work.

"Hi, Maria, wake up. Are you OK?" inquired her aunt, breaking the silence that surrounded Maria's contemplations.

Maria stirred from her slumber and mumbled a tired acknowledgment. Exhaustion and her monthly visitor had taken their toll.

"It's okay; I'll handle the cooking. Take some rest," her aunt reassured.

## CHAPTER 7

"Thanks," Selina replied before drifting back into a deep sleep.

The following day, Maria decided to investigate the mysterious phone number from the business card. She enlisted the help of her friend, Mantwa, who had a landline at home. Craftily, Maria handed Mantwa the number, claiming she wanted to check if it belonged to one of Kolobe's flings.

Mantwa agreed, seizing the opportunity while her parents were out. Maria dialed the number, concealing her voice with a handkerchief.

"Hello, who's calling?" came the voice of Peter Serumula.

"I'm calling from Wesbank. Before I proceed, may I confirm if I'm speaking with Mr. Peter Serumula?" Mantwa inquired.

"Yes, that's me. How can I assist you?" Peter Serumula responded.

"I got a call from WesBank about your overdue car payments," Mantwa said.

"Sorry, there must be a mistake. I don't have an account with WesBank," Peter Serumula replied, frustration evident in his voice.

"Yeah, I am, but I don't have any dealings with WesBank," Peter reiterated.

"Thanks for your patience," Mantwa said, hanging up.

Peter wondered, "Who is this person?" These institutions often dial wrong numbers.

Mantwa told Maria that the person on the phone confirmed he was Mr. Peter Serumula, a government employee. Maria sighed in relief; this was the client Pretty mentioned, paying big for services, and he was her father.

Sadly, it seemed Pretty didn't know the client's true identity. Maria thanked Mantwa for verifying the number.

"Why's that number so important?" Mantwa asked.

"It's crucial, but I'll fill you in later. Please don't discuss today's events with anyone," Maria pleaded.

"My lips are like a sealed tomb," Mantwa whispered.

They went their separate paths. On her way home, Maria thought about the puzzle ahead: What's the next step? A physical test, perhaps. But how to make it happen? Maria wondered to herself.

**The Acid Test**

Maria bumped into Pretty while she was enjoying lunch at a local restaurant.

# CHAPTER 7

"Is this your secret hideaway?" Maria quizzed.

"Kind of, my dear," replied Pretty.

"How's your business going?" Maria inquired.

"A bit slow," Pretty admitted. "Some clients are struggling financially due to job losses. The economic situation isn't great, you know."

"Could this be the time mentioned in Genesis 41:29-36?" Maria pondered.

"What's that?" Pretty asked.

"It talks about seven years of famine and seven years of plenty," Maria explained.

"Oh, I remember that story," Pretty chuckled. "But why are you asking about that and my business?"

"I need money to buy certain things for women, and my parents won't give me any," Maria shared.

"Why not ask your boyfriend?" Pretty suggested.

"I don't want to make a habit of asking money from a boyfriend. I'd rather find my own way to get it," Maria explained.

"Sure, why not loan you the money?" Pretty suggested.

"No, I can't pay it back," Maria declined.

"Okay, here's the deal. I'll arrange for someone to take my place, but," Pretty pointed at Maria, "not him," she warned.

"Got it," Maria nodded.

"I've got a meeting with a rich guy tomorrow. I'll tell him I've got a client from Lesotho, and you'll step in for me. If all goes well, you'll get around R3000," Pretty explained.

"Interesting. What's next?" Maria asked.

"Do you have any lingerie?" Pretty inquired.

"Nope," Maria replied.

"Alright, let's hit up an adult store. I'll get you some," Pretty said. Together, they picked out and bought red lingerie.

They agreed to meet the next day, two hours before the client arrived, at a secluded spot.

At the discreet location, Pretty introduced Maria to the owner and led her to the room for adult services. There, Pretty guided Maria on striking a seductive pose on the bed.

The room had a big light in the middle of the ceiling and two

## CHAPTER 7

smaller lights near the bed's headboard. The ceiling light was plain white, but the ones by the headboard had colorful bulbs and were always kept dim.

Pretty, the person in charge, shared that customers had a key to the room but needed to knock three times before coming in. Once the door opened, Maria had to be on the bed, looking attractive.

People usually came to the place pretending to have lunch or dinner. The staff, understanding the customers' real plans, secretly slipped a piece of paper with a room number onto their tray during the meal. After eating, customers sneaked away to the restrooms and found hidden stairs leading to the assigned room.

The following day, Pretty and Maria went into the room together, but Pretty soon left. She explained that she couldn't provide her services that night due to a personal issue and introduced Maria's replacement. The customer agreed, as long as the new person offered the same quality of service as Pretty. After this, Pretty went home, receiving R4000 from the customer (she would later give R3000 to Maria the next day).

Peter approached the room, gently rapped on the door thrice, and swung it open. The room was bathed in soft, muted light, creating a familiar ambiance. Maria reclined on the bed, dressed in a striking red lingerie, assuming a provocative pose that immediately captured Peter's attention. Her enticing figure, with its seductive curves, drew him in like a metal object responding to a magnetic force.

# BROTHEL

Peter's pulse quickened, and he took rapid breaths. Swiftly, he shed his clothes, keeping his back turned to maintain a sense of discretion. Turning around, he seated himself on the bed, beginning to explore Maria's form while removing her lingerie.

Once both were undressed, they found themselves completely exposed. Peter positioned himself above Maria, and they embraced each other intimately. As the moments passed, Maria reached over and flicked on the overhead light, bathing the room in brightness. Now fully illuminated, they could clearly see each other.

Suddenly, pandemonium erupted. Both found themselves in a compromising, unclothed situation, and for a brief moment, they stared at each other in shocked silence.

Neither said a word. The room was silent. The sound of a needle could be heard when it fell on the ground. This was the moment truth. Chickens came home to roast. Father was having sexual relationship with daughter.

Maria shoved her father aside and grabbed the dress to put on. Peter lay in bed, naked and staring at the ceiling, absorbed in the rhythm of his heartbeat. Eventually, he rose, gathered his clothes, and dressed while Maria observed silently.

"So, is this where you have your secret meetings, the ones you lied to Mom about?" Maria asked, her voice tinged with anger.

He sat on the edge of the bed, face in hands, offering no response.

## CHAPTER 7

"I asked you a question," Maria demanded. "Answer me."

"Where's the towel?" Peter inquired.

"Why do you need a towel?" Maria pressed.

Peter explained his intention to wash and clean himself.

"I want you to take my dirt home, let Mom smell the filth on her husband," Maria declared furiously.

"Now I have proof of your double life. Dr. Jekyll by day, Mr. Hyde by night. A respectable person in daylight and a devil at night. I'll tell Mom you slept with your own flesh and blood," Maria panted angrily.

"Please, don't. I'll do whatever you want," Peter begged.

"I don't want anything from you. All I want is for you to spill the beans to Mom about what you did today," Maria insisted. "If you don't, I will." With that, she exited the room and headed home.

"Besides," she continued, "during dinner at home, I might just sit right across from you and discreetly brush my feet against yours under the table. Or, I could decide to stroll into your room in the buff while you're with Mom. If she wonders why, I'll just tell her to ask you.

"You're aware of the consequences if Mom and the neighbors find out about what you did to me," she reminded him.

Peter stayed silent, burying his face in his hands.

"So, spill the beans to Mom, or what?" Maria inquired.

"Let me make things simple for you, should you not tell Mom within a month, I will come naked at night in your bedroom while in bed with Mom and ask you to have sex with me". Maria told him.

"No! No! Please you cannot do that, I am your father," Peter pleaded.

"Yes you are, Then why did you just have sex with me, your daughter? Maria asked.

"I had no idea it was you," Peter confessed.

"Don't let Pretty know I'm your daughter; she has no clue. I found out after she accidentally dropped your business card at a restaurant where we were having lunch. Also, Maria mentioned that Pretty shouldn't be blamed," Peter explained.

"How am I supposed to break this to Mom?" Father asked.

"That's your problem, not mine," Maria responded.

It was a tough situation for the father. Eventually, during one of their dinner conversations, he informed his wife that it was in her best interest not to meddle in Maria's love life, as she was old enough to take care of herself.

# CHAPTER 7

"Why the sudden change of heart?" Selina asked.

"Let's not discuss it. I just felt that we should let her do what she wants," Peter replied.

The next day, Maria and Pretty met. Pretty handed her R3000.

"How did it go?" Pretty asked.

"Well, I was scared because I've never done anything like this before," Maria admitted.

"Would you like to do it again?" Pretty inquired.

"No," Maria replied.

"Thanks for the cash; I'm finally getting something I've been eyeing. We'll catch up later," Maria said as she headed out.

Maria and Auntie

During breakfast, Maria and her aunt shared a table. Maria, usually chatty, was oddly quiet, taking slow bites.

"Maria, everything alright? Is there something on your mind that you'd like to talk about?" Auntie asked.

"I'm just tired. Maybe it's the period that's draining me," Maria replied.

"Okay. I forgot to mention, I let your mom know you're with me for a bit, and you'll head home later. She was concerned about you," Auntie informed.

"You did the right thing," Maria agreed.

"Why did you choose to stay with me?" Auntie questioned.

"I just needed a break to calm down," Maria answered.

"That's fine; you don't have to spill the details," Auntie reassured.

"I noticed you got home late last night. Were you with your boyfriend? What's his name, and where does he live?" Auntie inquired.

"Let's steer clear of discussing him. The world's a maze of uncertainties; today's friend might be tomorrow's foe. It's like politicians – today they share laughter, tomorrow they're bitter enemies," Maria shared, brushing off the topic. She explained her late arrival by mentioning a visit to friends.

"What's the game plan post-Form 5?" Aunt inquired. "Any thoughts on what you want to study?"

"Not entirely sure, but Medicine appeals to me. I aspire to be a Medical Doctor," Maria replied.

"That's my niece! I'm proud of you. Your successes will elevate our family name. We're here for you, supporting you every

# CHAPTER 7

step," Aunt expressed with pride.

Aunt delved into Maria's return plans, offering company if needed. Maria assured her she'd be heading home next week and that there was no need for Aunt to tag along.

## Chapter: 8

## SERMON

**Church Service**

On a lazy Saturday afternoon, Selina was happily humming a hymn as she busied herself preparing and ironing clothes for the upcoming Sunday church service, both for herself and her husband.

Meanwhile, Maria, draped in a pair of daringly short shorts, sprawled out on the sofa with her legs nonchalantly propped open. She was engrossed in a TV soap opera, munching on popcorn, completely absorbed in her own world. On the other side of the room, Maria's father sat at the table, immersed in

## CHAPTER: 8

reading the Bible. Maria couldn't help but notice her father stealing glances her way, so she teasingly shifted her legs in response.

When Selina finally finished her chores, she made her way to the dining room. Upon seeing Maria's posture, she gently reminded her daughter of proper decorum. She urged Maria to sit more modestly, emphasizing that girls shouldn't sit with their legs wide open, especially in front of family members.

Ignoring her mother's advice, Maria remained defiant and continued lounging in her carefree position. In an attempt to shift the conversation, Selina inquired about Maria's plans for attending church the next day.

"Are you joining us for church tomorrow, Maria?" Selina asked.

Maria, seemingly uninterested, replied, "Not sure, why do you ask?"

Selina, with a sense of importance, revealed the significance of the day. "It's a special occasion. Your father will be delivering a sermon. It's a family affair, and we should all attend to offer him moral and spiritual support," she explained.

"I'm not sure; we'll see tomorrow when I wake up," Maria replied.

"Are you okay? You seem troubled by something. I'm your mother; if something is bothering you, talk to me," Selina asked.

# SERMON

"I'm just fine. Okay, I will attend," Maria replied.

"That's my girl," Selina remarked.

Peter was quietly reading the Bible. On Sunday, everyone drove in silence to the church, listening to gospel music on the radio.

In the churchyard, Peter parked in his usual spot. He greeted some congregants nearby before heading to the minister's office.

"Good morning, Minister. It's great to be here today," Peter said.

"All is well by the grace of God," the minister replied. "What is your message today?"

"It comes from the Book of Ephesians, Chapter 4, Verse 32. I hope the congregation will like it," Peter replied.

"What's its theme?" the minister asked.

"Forgiveness," Peter replied.

"Why forgiveness?" the minister asked.

"People should be informed and reminded that forgiveness is not a sin or a sign of weakness or stupidity. If Jesus Christ forgave us, why don't we do the same for our brothers and sisters, and..." The minister stopped him and said it was enough.

# CHAPTER: 8

The church echoed with hymns as the congregation gathered, filling the air with their collective voices. The Minister and Peter strolled up to the podium.

"Hello, everyone! In the name of the Father, the Son, and the Holy Spirit, I welcome you to this sacred space," the Minister announced with a warm smile. "Today is a special day as we come together to praise and strengthen our connection with the Lord."

Turning to Peter, he continued, "Our guest today is Evangelist Peter, who will share the sermon. Please join me in welcoming him.

Peter stepped forward and spoke, "Thank you, Minister. As mentioned, it's indeed a wonderful day to be in God's house. Today's message revolves around the power of forgiveness, inspired by Ephesians 4:32, which encourages us to 'be kind and compassionate to one another, forgiving each other, just as in Christ God forgave you.'"

He went on, "In our world, forgiveness seems challenging as people grapple with hurt and pain. Often, they find it difficult to forgive those who have wronged them, caught in the grip of negativity. Interestingly, the act of forgiveness is beautifully illustrated by a Presidential pardon, where certain prisoners are forgiven by the President."

Let us strive for forgiveness, breaking free from the chains that bind us, just as God forgave us through Christ," Peter concluded, imparting a message of compassion and reconciliation to the attentive congregation.

# SERMON

As Christians, messengers of God's Word, it's our mission to share the teachings of the Gospel, just as Matthew 28:19 instructs us: "Go unto the world and teach all nations." We're called to promote forgiveness and encourage others to let go of grudges.

Let's join in prayer:

Dear Lord, examine my heart and reveal any lingering wounds I've tried to forgive on my own. I ask that you cover these hurts with your healing grace. Grant me the strength to forgive others as completely as you forgave me. In Jesus's Name, Amen.

The congregation united in song, expressing their faith through a hymn. The Minister concluded the Church service with a heartfelt prayer:

Through God's grace, our souls find healing in today's message. May God empower us with the protective armor to stand against the devil's schemes. Amen.

The minister expressed gratitude to the congregation for their presence at the Church service.

## Death of Kolobe's Mother

As they reached home, Selina's neighbor called and shared the sad news that Joyce had passed away.

"Whoa! Was she sick?" Selina inquired.

# CHAPTER: 8

"People say she had cervical cancer," the neighbor replied.

"By the Grace of God, may her soul rest in peace," Selina remarked.

Entering the house, she conveyed the news to her husband, Peter, and Maria.

"Do I know her?" Peter asked.

"Not sure. Her house is on the other side of our section. She was a nurse at the hospital," Selina explained.

(Unbeknownst to Maria, it was Kolbe's mother.)

After lunch, Maria went out to visit a friend who informed her about the sudden death of Kolbe's mother. She then remembered what her mother had mentioned to her father after returning from church.

Maria was devastated.

# CHAPTER 9

## CONFESSION

**Skeleton coming out of the Cupboard**

The confession of evil works is the first beginning of good works (Saint Augustine).

The memorial for Joyce Nkuna drew a crowd, with Selepe, Mollo, and Maria showing up to support Kolobe. However, Peter Serumula's wife couldn't make it, claiming she felt unwell with a bad headache.

# CHAPTER 9

Selina felt uneasy being there because she had been unfaithful to her husband, and they had a child together. Once back home, Peter changed into more comfortable clothes, settled on the couch, and played Jim Reeve's songs on a vinyl record. He found himself repeatedly listening to the track, "Where Do I Go from Here?"

As the lyrics played, "Where do I go from here? What fate is coming near? Touch my hand and guide my lips in prayer…", Selina woke up and joined Peter. Curious, she asked about the funeral.

Peter shared that it was well-attended by senior managers from the Department of Health and nurses dressed in their traditional white uniforms. Concerned, Selina inquired about the cause of Joyce's death.

"I'm not sure, but people said she had cervical cancer," Peter replied.

"Aah! We're all destined to face the inevitable end someday, one way or another. Let's just be grateful that we're still breathing," Selina sighed.

"True, but it's important to cleanse our souls while we're here on earth," Peter chimed in.

Selina looked intrigued. "What do you mean by that?" she asked.

"God doesn't want sinners or those who harbor secrets," Peter explained.

Without directly responding to Peter, Selina shared, "I read in another book that some people die in spirit and others in flesh."

"What's the difference? Death is death, isn't it?" Peter questioned.

"Dying in spirit means being distant from God, while dying in flesh means your soul leaves your body, leaving behind a lifeless shell," Selina clarified.

"Wow, that's interesting," Peter remarked.

"As an evangelist, you should be aware of these things," Selina pointed out.

"Well, it's true, but we don't know everything. We're constantly learning, discovering new things every day. Like now, I've learned something I didn't know before," Peter replied.

**The Secrets**

Selina headed to the bathroom, and upon her return, she asked Peter to turn off the music. She needed to discuss something serious and sensitive with him. Peter, agreeing to her request, turned off the music. Selina took a deep breath, unsure of where to begin. In her heart, she thought, "What would be your reaction? However, thereafter, my soul shall be relieved."

## CHAPTER 9

Peter, sensing her seriousness, asked, "You are scaring me. What is it?"

"I am also scared," Selina admitted. Then, she began to reveal a painful truth:

"During the times you were away for work training overseas, something terribly sinful and morally unacceptable happened."

"What is that?" Peter inquired, his concern growing.

"I was lonely," Selina confessed. "There were moments when I longed for love. With you not returning my calls, the idea that you might be having an affair crossed my mind. One day, I met a man. As the days went by, we became intimate. Unfortunately, during your last visit before coming home for good, I discovered that I was pregnant."

I didn't tell you about what happened because I was scared you'd leave me, and I kept quiet to protect your standing in the Church. I thought about ending the pregnancy, but the doctors advised against it. A few months after you came back, I finally told you. I knew you couldn't deny it because we were intimate before your last return – it wasn't you, though, as I was on the pill.

After you left, I made a mistake and got pregnant after sleeping with someone else without protection. The child, Maria, is the result of that. Her father is the father of her boyfriend, the same man you saw at her funeral today. Maria and Selepe don't know, and the woman who passed away had no idea about me.

What's more, Maria and Kolobe don't know they're siblings.

"Is that why you didn't attend the funeral?" Peter asked.

"Yes. I felt guilty attending the funeral of someone I betrayed."

"That's all I needed to tell you."

"I'm at a loss for words. May God guide us through this challenging time," Peter sighed.

"There's something I need to confess," he continued.

"Upon returning home for the last time, I couldn't bear your sudden reluctance to be intimate with me. I didn't want to resort to self-pleasure, nor did I want to pressure you, fearing it could lead to false accusations. I confided in a friend about my bedroom struggles, and he suggested a brothel.

I began visiting the place, often using work meetings as an excuse. I wanted to quit, but found myself unable to break free. One day, my regular companion couldn't provide the service, so she brought in friends, claiming they were from Lesotho. I agreed.

"Oh, my God," Peter paused, tears streaming down his face. "I never knew that the girl from Lesotho was someone we knew..."

He took a moment to compose himself before continuing.

## CHAPTER 9

"It turned out to be Maria. We were both undressed, and I slept with her."

Selina, trying to provide comfort, said, "It's okay, don't cry." Little did she know the shocking revelation that was about to unfold.

Maria threatened me, saying she'd stroll into our bedroom bare if I didn't spill the beans to you. I was clueless about breaking the news to you.

They both stayed silent, exchanging disbelieving glances. Eventually, a hug bridged the gap, and forgiveness flowed.

Selina and Peter pardoned each other, opting to move forward as if the hiccup never occurred. Selina wisely suggested keeping Maria in the dark until after her crucial Grade 12 exams, so as not to disrupt her preparation.

She planned to later inform Maria about the past indiscretions, expressing forgiveness, and revealing details about her biological father. However, the brothel incident was to remain a secret from Selepe. Selina emphasized the universal truth that humans make mistakes, unlike animals, and one's position in life doesn't exempt them from errors.

Political leaders, educators, nurses, pastors, lawyers, and community leaders often find themselves in challenging situations. Despite this, they strive to avoid engaging in immoral and regrettable actions.

They are determined not to be lured into wrongdoing, as they understand the consequences it might have in the future. They firmly believe that intentionally committing a wrongful act and then seeking forgiveness afterwards is both unacceptable and immoral.

It's crucial to recognize that certain actions are not mere mistakes; they are deliberate choices made with full awareness of their potential outcomes. Engaging in unprotected sex or consorting with prostitutes, for example, is not accidental; rather, it is a purposeful and conscious decision.

*What distinguishes humans from animals is their capacity for critical thinking. This cognitive ability empowers humans to consider the consequences of their actions. Every action undertaken by humans is a conscious and thoughtful choice.*

# CHAPTER 10

## PREPARATIONS

### Life Skills

In the City Council Library of Mamelodi, there was a remarkable librarian. This was in the days before the library faced the unfortunate fate of being burned down during the upheavals of 1976. Undeterred by challenges, the librarian, along with fellow academics, decided to create something positive for the community.

During the three to four weeks of winter school holidays, students found themselves with a lot of free time on their hands. This prompted the birth of Life Skills workshops. The goal was

# PREPARATION

simple: to engage the students in meaningful activities that went beyond the regular school curriculum. These workshops aimed to equip them for life after school and help them navigate the challenges of university, technikon, and life in general.

Twice a week, students gathered voluntarily for these sessions, where they delved into a variety of important topics. The workshops covered everything from understanding and preventing sexually transmitted diseases to avoiding unplanned pregnancies. They explored the dangers of smoking and drug use, the health risks associated with alcoholism, and the long-term effects of bullying.

But the learning didn't stop there. The workshops emphasized the significance of respect for parents, delving into the complexities of parenting itself. Students were also taught practical skills, such as how to write compelling applications for university admission or employment opportunities.

The cornerstone of these teachings was the theory of "The Jellybeans," highlighting the importance of respect and obedience for parents. In this creative and caring environment, the librarian and the academics aimed to plant the seeds of wisdom that would grow with the students throughout their lives, helping them navigate the challenges that lay ahead.

There was a theory that said, "When someone steps into a magical park, a Bear appears. This Bear, at first, is quite unfriendly and has a strong desire to harm the person. However, if the person offers the Bear Jellybeans, something amazing happens – the Bear's mood changes, and it happily embraces the person. But here's the catch: if the person runs out of Jellybeans, the Bear turns dangerous and, sadly, takes their life."

Now, imagine children as these Bears. They, too, have a tendency to ask for countless things from their parents. When parents can't fulfill these wishes, the children might get upset, throw tantrums, and even resort to emotional blackmail, making their parents feel as if they're on the edge of a cliff.

In Proverbs 29:15, it is wisely said, "The rod of correction imparts wisdom, but a child left to himself disgraces his mother." This suggests that a bit of discipline goes a long way in raising a child properly.

Parenting is like being in a special club where parents need to stand firm and tall to guide their children. It's not about creating a hierarchy where some are more important than others, like in the animal farm. Parents shouldn't get disheartened and complain that their children are unruly.

Parents who neglect their moral duties might find themselves shouting at their children, saying things like:

"Look at me, I always listened to my parents."

"I had great respect for my parents."

So, in the grand adventure of parenting, let's remember the magical Jellybeans of love, guidance, and understanding to ensure our Bears (children) always have smiles and hugs to share.

Back in the day, this person didn't appreciate their parents

# PREPARATION

when they were young. Now, their own kids are giving them a taste of their own medicine.

A newborn in the family is like a precious gem. It can either bring joy or sadness to the family and society. But, for that child to become a well-behaved adult, the parent must not ignore their moral duties. It's like cooking a meal – even with fresh veggies, meat, the right pot, temperature, and a good mix, if it tastes bad, it's on the cook.

If the dish is unsavory, who's to blame? The cook, of course!

Also, folks discovered that money isn't the only key to happiness. People are born into different economic situations, be it rich or poor. It's up to each person to change their socio-economic status.

So, plant a tree today, nurture it with deep, sturdy roots, and later on, you'll enjoy the sweet fruits it bears.

**Back at school**

The deadline for the Form 5 (Grade 12) final exams was looming, and stress was on the rise. No time for fun outside of school, as everyone was caught up in exam preparations.

Teachers were working tirelessly, buzzing around like busy bees, focusing on revisions. Mock exams were taken to gauge the students' readiness, and the results weren't promising. There were issues with answering questions and properly analyzing stories from the textbooks.

## CHAPTER: 10

In response, teachers tried various revision methods to assist students in reading, understanding, and answering questions correctly, as well as analyzing stories from the textbooks.

Amidst this academic frenzy, a man took a stroll by the riverbank one day. Weary, he decided to rest under a tree's shade near the river and dozed off.

During his nap, he had a dream. In this dream, he found himself walking along a riverbank and witnessed someone attempting to cross the river. The crossing seemed shallow, but tragically, the person fell into the water and struck a submerged rock. In his dream, the man leaped into the river to rescue the drowning person, only to find that the person was already lifeless.

As he opened his eyes, a colossal tree limb, sheltering him during his slumber, crashed down and claimed his life.

"Whoa! What an incredible, mind-bending tale," exclaimed a student.

The teacher inquired, "Did you enjoy the story?"

"Oh yes, it's amazing," replied the students in unison.

"Is the story believable?" questioned the teacher.

"Yes," confidently answered Kolobe.

The teacher turned to Letlapa, "What about you?"

"I am not sure," hesitated Letlapa.

"Kolobe, you said yes. But have you considered how a deceased person could share this story?" the teacher probed.

"I never thought about that," admitted Kolobe.

The teacher continued, "Who witnessed this man strolling by the riverbank?"

"Who did he confide in about the dream?" the teacher pressed on.

"And to whom did he reveal that he initially perished in his dream, preceding his real demise under the tree branch?" the teacher questioned.

The teacher concluded, "Such narratives are meant to make us ponder. They encourage us to think beyond the obvious and not blindly accept everything we hear from others."

He insisted that many kids fail exams not because they're clueless about the subjects, but because they don't put in the effort to grasp the questions. He also emphasized that every story carries a message. As the reader, it's your job to delve into the lines, grasp the author's message, and interpret it.

The tale I just shared may seem simple, but it underscores the significance of comprehension and interpretation.

The teacher, who had previously appeared on TV and dis-

# CHAPTER: 10

cussed educational programs on Radio Thobela, decided to test the class's ability to answer a question. With enthusiasm, the teacher asked, "Do any of you know me?" Hands shot up in excitement.

Pointing to one student, the teacher inquired, "Yes, what's your answer?" The student replied, "I recognize you because I heard you speak on certain educational programs on both TV and the Radio."

The teacher then turned to the rest of the class and asked, "What about the rest of you? Any answers?"

The classroom lay silent, so hushed that it seemed even the faintest sound, like a falling nail, could be heard. The teacher spoke, "I didn't inquire about where you know me from. I asked, 'Do you know me?'"

Adding on, the teacher explained that the question had two parts: "Part One - Do you know me? The answer is 'Yes.' Part Two - How do you know me? The response would be, 'I once heard you speaking on the radio during educational programs.'"

To dispel students' apprehension, motivational speakers, including church ministers, were invited every Friday to address the students. They emphasized that education and knowledge go beyond mere repetition, urging students to apply what they learn to shape not only their lives but also the lives of others and the community.

As the students sat for their final examinations, the results

# PREPARATION

were later published in local newspapers the following January. Many students excelled, achieving more than a 65% average.

With the culmination of Form 5 (Grade 12), it became a faded memory as the journey to tertiary education unfolded. Around the end of January, Selepe was released from prison, marking a new chapter in the unfolding story.

# CHAPTER 11

## CONVERSATIONS

In January, as students feverishly reached out to universities and technikons in pursuit of further education, Selina and Maria found themselves deep in conversation one Sunday after church.

Seated on the veranda, Selina began, "I've called you to discuss something important."

A worried Maria responded, "You're scaring me. What's going on?"

"Firstly, congratulations to you on your outstanding exam

results. Your father and I are proud," Selina praised.

"Thank you, and I appreciate your support," Maria replied.

Selina, with a serious tone, continued, "What I want to discuss is quite sensitive, and I hope you'll take it in the right spirit."

She sighed before explaining, "You see, the surface may be calm, like the beautiful water you observe flowing smoothly. However, beneath it, there are hidden creatures that can cause harm or even be deadly. Life has its share of such elements."

Recalling her commitment, Selina said, "When I married your father, I vowed to stand by him through thick and thin."

"Maria anxiously questioned, 'For God's sake, what are you talking about?'

Selina shared her worry about her father not returning her calls sometimes. The suspicion that he might be involved with another woman fueled her fear. Little did she know that when fear takes over, faith tends to fade away.

Adding to her concerns, Selina mentioned Psalm 24:5, where God reminds us that doubts and fears are enemies. However, she admitted succumbing to the devil's influence, letting go of faith and engaging in something devastating.

Maria, desperate for clarity, pressed, 'Come to the point, what did you do?'

CHAPTER: 11

Selina revealed a secret from many years ago when Maria's father went to Germany for a three-year study assignment. He would come home for a week once or twice a year. Feeling lonely during his absence, Selina sought companionship and intimacy. She met a man, and what started as a friendly relationship escalated to a physical one. She confessed that during Maria's father's last week-long visit before returning for good the following year around March, they had been intimate about three times."

After he came back to Germany, I ended up sleeping with him.

"What's his name, and where does he live?" Maria inquired.

"I'll tell you later," I replied. Soon after, we shared moments of intimacy about three times, and I was oblivious to the fact that I wasn't on contraception. Before I knew it, I found myself pregnant. Wanting to terminate the pregnancy, I consulted doctors who advised against it due to my health condition.

"You did what? You, a professional nurse, forgot the pill?" Maria exclaimed, panting. "I don't understand. You're the one who always emphasizes to young girls that they must never forget to take the pill and, if forgetful, opt for an injection."

"Well, it was a mistake; that's why the word 'forgetful' exists," I explained. "But that doesn't justify my error."

When your father returned, I didn't disclose my involvement with this man. I only informed him about the pregnancy. Surprisingly, he was happy, thinking it was a result of our numerous intimate encounters before he returned to Germany. I felt relieved.

"But that's adultery," Maria pointed out.

"Yes, and I am not proud of it," Selina admitted with a heavy heart.

Maria, puzzled, asked, "Why are you telling me all these things?"

Tears streamed down Selina's face as she replied, "I want you to know the truth because I can't keep this secret anymore."

"This man I am talking about is..." Selina paused, overcome with emotion. Maria handed her a tissue to wipe away the tears. "This man is your father."

"What?" Maria exclaimed, her emotions escalating. "My father? What on earth are you talking about?"

With a heavy sigh, Selina confirmed, "Yes, he is your father. His name is James Nku, and Kolobe is his son."

Maria, incredulous, protested, "What are you talking about? Mr. James Nku is the father of Kolobe, my boyfriend?" She panted, trying to make sense of the shocking revelation.

Selina sadly nodded, "Yes, I'm afraid that is the truth."

## CHAPTER: 11

"I don't believe you. This is ridiculous; it cannot be true. Kolobe, my boyfriend?" Maria questioned in disbelief.

They fell into a momentary silence. Selina then went inside the house and returned with a large envelope, saying, "Before I talk about the documents inside this envelope..."

In hushed tones, I shared the brothel incident with my husband, hashing out the details between him and me, and the recent revelation with you. We chose to bury the hatchet, forgive each other, and move forward as if the incident had never occurred. My husband extended an apology to you. We made a pact not to disclose the brothel matter to Selepe, focusing only on informing him about his father.

Maria's response was a heavy silence, tears streaming down her face. Overwhelmed, she rose from her seat, clutching her head in disbelief. "What is happening in this world?" she questioned. "Why do people commit wrongs and then blame the devil?" Panting and shouting, her gaze at me resembled that of a starving animal.

Selina remained silent, tears falling.

Maria, struggling to comprehend, asked, "Why keep such a weighty secret all these years?" Selina explained that she was safeguarding the family's reputation, aiming to prevent a divorce.

Maria's voice trembled, "I've heard people talk about a devil, and you, you're the devil." With that, she stood up, crying uncontrollably, and retreated into her bedroom, slamming the door shut. Selina, too, wept in the aftermath of the emotional storm.

One evening, Selina entered her bedroom, holding an envelope that contained important documents. She asked Maria to join her for a discussion about the contents. Maria assured her that she could explain the documents.

"Before we delve into this, please forgive me for my mistakes," Selina apologized for her past actions.

"Whether I forgive you or not, what's done is done. Time cannot be turned back. I forgive you," Maria responded with grace.

Selina began to explain the contents of the documents. "These papers prove that James Nku has been making deposits since your birth. It's to fund your university education. And here is the Education Policy from Peter Serumula, my husband."

Curious, Maria asked, "Has James Nku, the man I thought was my father, seen me?"

Selina nodded. "Yes, I shared your photos with him from your infancy to now. You're free to meet him if you wish."

"That's alright. I'll continue to stay in this house and consider you and Peter Serumula as my parents. But what about Kolobe? How will he know we're half-siblings?" Maria inquired.

# CHAPTER: 11

"I've asked his father to inform him. It's taken care of," Selina assured her. They shared a moment of understanding as the complexities of their relationships unfolded.

**James Nku and Kolobe**

"Dad, I aced Grade 12! I'm so grateful for your support," James happily told Kolobe.

"Thanks a bunch, Dad. Your belief in me means everything," Kolobe replied with a smile.

"So, what's the plan for college?" James inquired.

"I want to dive into law," Kolobe shared.

"Wow! That's fantastic! Have you applied anywhere?" James asked eagerly.

"Yep, got into the University of Pretoria," Kolobe revealed.

"That's amazing! Don't stress about tuition; I've saved up, plus there's the Education Policy. Your studies are sorted," assured James.

"Thanks for the awesome news. I was worried about the money, but this is a relief," Kolobe admitted.

But then, James hinted at something important. "There's something I need to share, something sensitive."

"I'm all ears," Kolobe responded, curious.

Years ago, your mom and I had a big disagreement because she didn't want to be close with me. It made me do something wrong—I got involved with someone else and she got pregnant. That's how Maria came into the picture, and she happens to be your girlfriend. It turns out, you and Maria share the same dad, me, making you half-siblings. So, falling in love isn't an option.

I've already let Maria know about this, and I'm truly sorry for the mess," James confessed.

"Whoa! This is unbelievable. Are you serious?" Kolobe asked.

"Yeah, it's true," James confirmed.

"Well, what's done is done," Kolobe sighed, tears welling up in his eyes.

"I understand it's tough to swallow, but it's the reality," James said.

**Selepe**

Peter broke the surprising news to Selepe that Maria wasn't his daughter, but rather the daughter of James Nku, who also happened to be Kolobe's father. (Not to mention any details about the brothel issue.)

He went on to explain that his mother and James Nku had

## CHAPTER: 11

thoroughly discussed the circumstances of Maria's birth. Despite any initial challenges, they had forgiven each other and decided not to pursue a divorce. Instead, they agreed to carry on with their lives as if nothing had happened.

Kolobe, taken aback, exclaimed, "Good heavens! Is that true?"

Peter affirmed, "Yes, it's true, my son." He reassured Kolobe, "I will continue to embrace Maria as my daughter, and I hope you'll continue to see her as your younger sister."

In response, Selepe said, "Yes, father. The status quo shall remain."Thank you, my son, for your understanding," Peter expressed his gratitude.

**Maria and Selepe**

Maria and Selepe bumped into each other and started chatting about the serious talk their parents had with them. They decided to be like family forever. Maria happily shared her big news with Selepe—she got accepted into Medical School!

Adding to the excitement, she mentioned that she had the funds from her scholarship and some help from her dad (the details of which Selepe didn't delve into). Knowing that jobs were tough for him, Maria thought it would be awesome to get him a car. This way, he could use it as a taxi and make a living.

Selepe couldn't contain his joy. They both shared the fantastic news with their parents, who were just as thrilled about this newfound brother-sister bond.

**Maria and Kolobe**

Before embarking on their separate journeys to university, they gathered to share the startling revelations their parents had disclosed. This meeting, however, was far from the usual ones; now, they faced each other not as lovers but as half-siblings.

The weight of the situation was palpable, and there seemed to be no remedy for the spilled water of their past love. In a silent exchange of glances, Kolobe broke the quietude, acknowledging that harboring hatred was futile. Instead, he suggested they move forward, casting aside the shadows of their romantic history, and embrace their new roles as brother and sister. Maria concurred, sealing their commitment with a heartfelt embrace.

As they planned their academic pursuits, Maria revealed her path to Witwatersrand University for Medicine, while Kolobe shared his destination at the University of Pretoria for Law. In a joint decision, they opted to keep their transformed relationship a secret from their friends, choosing to present themselves as caring siblings instead.

Their story unfolded alongside those of other friends who, too, ventured into university life, pursuing degrees in various fields.

# CONSEQUENCES OF THE HOUSE OF DECEITS

### LETLAPA

In the House of Hardships, there lived an extraordinary Eagle Family. Little Letlapa, right from his early days, learned the importance of shouldering responsibilities and reaching for the skies to make his dreams come true.

Despite facing initial challenges, he never gave up. Through unwavering dedication and wholehearted commitment, Letlapa turned his struggles into stepping stones. Surprisingly, the naysayers, who tried to throw him off course, unintentionally fueled his determination, propelling him to soar higher and higher.

### MARIA

Maria triumphantly completed her medical studies, earning herself an MBCHB degree. For the next two years, she dedicated her time to an internship at the local hospital. However, her journey took an unexpected turn when she decided to set up her practice in a semi-rural area, approximately 110km from Mamelodi.

Quietly embarking on this new chapter, Maria didn't inform her parents of the specific location. She assured them she'd reach out once she was settled. Unattached romantically, she secured a modest two-room house not far from her clinic. Evenings were spent immersed in medical research journals and the drama of love stories on TV before retiring for the night.

The semi-rural area was rapidly developing but lacked sufficient medical professionals and a proper hospital, featuring only a small clinic. Maria's relocation aimed to establish herself and generate funds. However, the patient influx fell short, with some days passing without a single visitor. The residents, primarily subsistence farmers and industrial workers, posed a unique challenge. Thankfully, the area boasted minimal crime.

In an effort to supplement her practice, Maria attempted to secure a part-time position at the local clinic. Unfortunately, her plans were thwarted by budget constraints; the government couldn't allocate funds for two doctors. Undeterred, Maria navigated the delicate balance between her aspirations and the challenges of the developing community she had chosen to serve.

The cholera outbreak swept through the area, filling hospitals with patients, but its impact was short-lived. The small town, adorned with a handful of shops, a couple of restaurants, a police station, a fire station, and a Municipality Office, was nestled between a village and an urban expanse. Amidst this, a captivating nature resort beckoned, hosting annual Music Festivals that drew artists from Mamelodi and Johannesburg.

In the midst of this seemingly tranquil setting, a young woman found herself haunted by recurring nightmares. These dreams replayed a disturbing incident from her past, revealing that the man she thought was her father was, in fact, a stepfather. The dreams took a twisted turn as she experienced an intimate relationship with him, leaving her unsettled. This tormenting vision recurred every fortnight, and she grappled with the distress alone, reluctant to confide in anyone or seek professional help. Though she initially turned to tranquilizers for relief, she wisely halted before succumbing to addiction.

As news of the upcoming Music Festival reached her, a spark of excitement ignited within her. The prospect of music soothing her frayed nerves and offering respite from the nightmares enticed her. Perhaps, amidst the melodies, she hoped to find solace and, just maybe, discover someone to love. Feeling the urgency to embrace romance, marriage, and family life, she adorned herself in elegant attire, packed a cooler bag with cold drinks, and set off for the festival.

The festival grounds buzzed with people from various places, all converging for the love of music. Amidst the crowd, she noticed a couple, slightly apart from the rest—a Black girl and a White man—sharing moments of affection through occasional kisses. The diversity of love on display amid the music festival's vibrant atmosphere left an indelible mark on her, offering a glimmer of hope for a future free from the haunting shadows of her nightmares.

Maria found herself intrigued by the activities around her.

"When will I find someone to love me?" she pondered quietly.

"Well, one day it will happen," she assured herself.

The bathrooms were just a few meters away from where she was sitting, and patrons on their way there passed in front of her. Among them was a black girl who caught Maria's attention. The girl whispered something into the ear of her white boyfriend, and he playfully patted her buttocks. She was dressed in a revealing short outfit as she strolled towards the bathroom. Maria recognized her immediately.

"What on earth are you doing here?" Maria inquired.

The girl turned out to be Pretty, a friend from back home.

"I should be asking you the same question," Pretty replied.

"I'm staying in this village now," Maria explained.

"Okay, let me quickly go and pee," Pretty said, hurrying off to the bathroom. Upon her return, she kindly helped Maria carry her cooler bag and rejoined her boyfriend.

"Hi, sweetheart, this is Maria, my best friend from Mamelodi," Pretty introduced Maria to her boyfriend, Eric.

Additionally, Pretty shared that Eric was not only her boyfriend but also a Research Engineer originally from Switzerland.

"How do you do?" Eric greeted.

"I'm okay," Maria responded with a friendly smile.

"My sweetheart shared tales of you, mentioning that since you departed Mamelodi, your name echoed in her ears," Eric remarked.

"Indeed, I wanted to escape Mamelodi and embark on a new journey, on my own," Maria replied.

Pretty interrupted the conversation, suggesting they immerse themselves in the music. The DJ played Letta Mbuli's song, "Maru A Pula" (Clouds of Rain), a widely loved tune. Pretty gracefully stood up and danced, showcasing her proficiency in multiple body styles.

As the song concluded, Maria applauded. "Wow! Your diverse dance moves are impressive," Maria remarked.

"Oh, I'm just trying my best," Pretty modestly replied.

Maria checked her watch, announcing that it was time for her to leave and prepare for the next day. Eric suggested they should also depart, considering the distance they had to cover to get home. They gathered their belongings and headed to the parking area.

Pretty and Eric approached a two-door red convertible Alpha Romeo. "Maria, meet my baby. Eric got it for me about two months ago," Pretty proudly told Maria.

"Seriously? That's amazing!" Maria exclaimed.

"No joke, I'm serious," Pretty confirmed.

"Some folks have luck, others don't," Maria remarked.

"It's true, just like in Animal Farm. All animals are equal, but some are more equal than others," Eric added.

"Well, you guys should come visit me someday. We can relax and have a good time together," Maria suggested with a warm smile.

"That sounds like a great plan; we'll definitely honor the invitation," Pretty exclaimed with enthusiasm as they all bid farewell.

About a month later, Maria got a call informing her that Pretty would be coming to visit. Confirming the visit, Maria eagerly awaited the day. When Pretty, Eric, and Eric's friend Michael from Denmark, a Chemical Engineer, finally arrived, the atmosphere was delightful.

Meeting someone for the first time always brings a sense of hope and adventure. As Eric introduced Michael to Maria, her eyes sparkled with admiration, and her heart raced. "It's my pleasure and honor to meet you," said Michael.

"The pleasure is mine," Maria responded, her hand trembling with joy as she shook his. Love seemed to blossom at first sight, a fact not lost on Pretty, who promptly suggested they talk privately.

"Look me in the eyes. You seem to like or love this guy. Do you?" Pretty asked Maria.

"It appears so. Perhaps I am foolish to say that," Maria admitted.

"Follow your heart, my dear," Pretty advised.

Deciding it was time for a barbecue, they gathered for a braai. Michael took charge of grilling, Eric tended to the fire, while Maria and Pretty marinated the meat. After a delicious meal accompanied by semi-sweet wine and soft music, Maria played Elton John's "Lady in Red." Maria was dressed in sexy red shorts, and Pretty wore alluring white shorts, creating a memorable evening filled with warmth and connection.

"Michael quizzed Maria, 'What did you study in school?'

'Medicine,' she replied.

'Where?' he inquired.

'University of Witwatersrand,' Maria shared.

'What are you up to now?' Michael continued his questions.

'I run my own private practice in this village,' Maria answered.

'Wow, that's impressive. Many doctors prefer big cities,' Michael remarked.

'And you?' Maria turned the conversation, asking about him.

'I'm a Chemical Engineer, graduated in Denmark, my hometown. Currently working at a research center in South Africa,' Michael explained.

'Great, contributing to our country,' Maria praised.

Deciding it was time to loosen up, Maria played Chris de Burgh's 'The Lady in Red.' When she returned, she asked Michael for a dance, and he agreed. Pretty and Eric followed suit.

During the dance, Michael whispered the song lyrics into Maria's ear as she rested her head on his shoulder. The atmosphere was charged, and love seemed to envelop them.

After the dance, Pretty and Eric discreetly retreated to a corner, giving Maria and Michael some privacy. Michael didn't mince words, expressing his admiration for Maria's beauty and intelligence. He confessed his love, assuring her she could take her time to respond.

Maria agreed to contemplate the matter. As night fell, they bid farewell, leaving Maria alone with her thoughts. Surprisingly, there were no nightmares that night. Her mind was consumed by the memory of dancing with Michael, and thoughts of him lingered as she drifted into a peaceful sleep."

The lyrics

*"The lady in red is dancing with me, cheek to cheek,*

*There is nobody here, it's just you and me.*

*It's where I want to be"*

These lyrics were occasionally in her mind.

"I think I'm in love with Michael. Is that normal, or am I fooling myself?" Maria pondered.

The next day, she called up Pretty to check on their recent trip.

"Hey, my friend! We had a safe journey. I've got something to spill—Michael is head over heels for you. He wants you to be his girlfriend and eventually his wife," Pretty excitedly shared with Maria.

"Okay, but I haven't decided whether to accept his proposal," Maria replied.

"Just take your time. Michael mentioned he wants to visit you alone before the end of the month," Pretty added.

"That sounds great," Maria responded.

Sure enough, before the month was up, they met and confirmed their love. Michael suggested Maria should move to the CBD, offering to help find a place to live and a job since it was too far and risky for him to travel there regularly.

A few months later, Maria relocated to the CBD without her parents knowing her whereabouts.

"It's amazing how someone can break your heart, and you can still love them with all the little pieces." - Ella Harper.

In the following year, Maria and Michael's love story surpassed that of Romeo and Juliet. They explored various parts of South Africa, cherishing every moment together. Maria finally felt she had found a soulmate, and her bad nightmares disappeared.

One Saturday, Pretty urgently called Maria, insisting on a meeting. Without hesitation, they agreed to meet in town.

Maria arrived first, and when Pretty showed up, she was in a sorry state—poorly dressed, with worn-out clothes. Maria couldn't believe her eyes.

"Hey! What happened to you?" Maria desperately asked.

Pretty poured out her heart, sharing the painful tale of her departed love, Eric, who not only left her emotionally shattered but also drove away with her car. Stranded without money or a stable place to call home, she resorted to surviving on handouts, her thoughts even darkening with the notion of suicide.

Maria, wide-eyed and empathetic, responded with genuine concern. "Oh no, that's devastating. I'm at a loss for words. Stay with me for now, until things get better," she offered.

"Thank you so much," Pretty replied, gratitude evident in her eyes.

After a quiet lunch, they made their way to Maria's place. Silence enveloped them during the journey, each lost in her own thoughts. As they approached Maria's residence, a quote echoed in Pretty's mind: "It is strange, but true, that the most important turning points of life often come at the most unexpected times and in the most unexpected ways" (Napoleon Hill).

Upon reaching Maria's building, they entered the elevator, bound for the second floor where Maria's suite awaited. However, a surprising discovery awaited them as they stood before Maria's door—a conspicuous notice that left them both puzzled and intrigued.

"Locked out, two months behind on rent," the notice on Maria's door declared. She made her way down to the Reception Area, sinking into a sofa. Dialling Michael, she braced herself for his response.

His voice, sharp and irritated, barked, "What?"

"It's Maria. I've been locked out. There's a notice about two months of rent due," she explained.

"Pay up if you want to stay. I'm not running a charity," he retorted.

"But you could have warned me about the rent," Maria pleaded.

Michael's tone turned indifferent. "Lost interest, my dear. Like ice melting in my mouth. You're young, beautiful, educated. You'll find someone suitable."

"What have I done wrong? Left out in the cold without a blanket?" Maria questioned.

"This conversation leads nowhere. I forgot to mention—I'm married. My wife was in the hospital when we met. Now she's recovered, and we're going home. I have no reason to leave her for you. Don't call me again. I've paid the rent arrears, and you must pay up," he stated before abruptly ending the call."

Maria couldn't fathom why Michael had suddenly turned against her. She pondered over what mistakes she might have made and why he hadn't communicated them to her. The revelation of Michael's marriage hit her like a bolt from the blue, and she struggled to find any answers.

Feeling overwhelmed, Maria retreated to the bedroom, where

her sobs caught the attention of her friend Pretty. Concerned, Pretty approached and inquired about the source of Maria's distress.

"Why the tears? What's going on?" Pretty asked.

"It's Michael. He doesn't love me anymore and told me not to contact him," Maria replied.

"Troubles never come alone. Let's go to the dining room, watch TV, and talk about these issues once you've calmed down. It seems like these guys have left us hanging," Pretty suggested.

In the dining room, as they watched TV, Maria couldn't keep her emotions in check any longer. She questioned Pretty about the fairness and unfairness of life, especially for those uninterested in prosperity.

Maria then shared a secret with Pretty, recounting the day they met at a restaurant during a school holiday. She confessed to finding a business card in Pretty's bag, revealing a lucrative client who turned out to be Maria's father, unbeknownst to her at the time.

Pretty, taken aback, nodded in acknowledgment. Maria continued, disclosing that the client was not her biological father. Pretty's eyes widened in shock.

"Really?" Pretty exclaimed.

"Yes," Maria affirmed. "The silver lining is that there was no physical intimacy, but the darkness is that we saw each other's bodies. I never told my mother or anyone else, keeping it a secret. However, as the years passed, nightmares haunted me, featuring a more intense and disturbing version of that incident."

After my boyfriend's mother passed away, shocking revelations surfaced. My own mother disclosed to me that my boyfriend's father was, in fact, my biological father. The man I had been intimate with was not my real dad. I was devastated, tears streaming down my face. The person I deeply loved turned out to be my half-brother, and the man I had respected as my father was not my biological parent.

I can't blame Pretty; she had no idea about all this at the time.

Later, I discovered that my mother had denied my supposed father his marital rights because he frequented brothels. Deception had infiltrated my family – a secret child, a father visiting brothels, and children who believed they shared the same parents but didn't.

It seemed like the legacy of deceit had been passed down to us, their children. Here I am, trying to build a life, only to have my dreams shattered by the lies that surrounded me.

"Oh God, what should I do? Is my life so worthless that I should consider ending it?" Maria cried out in despair.

"I don't know what to say, my friend," Pretty was utterly shocked by Maria's revelation.

They sat in silence for a moment, the only sounds being the faint hum of the TV and distant voices outside. Around 8:00 PM, they went to bed. Pretty suggested they pray before sleeping, but Maria rejected the idea, feeling it wasn't worth it. So, they drifted off to sleep without a prayer.

The next day, a lazy Sunday sun cast its warm glow over the small kitchen. They rustled up a simple breakfast of eggs, avocado, baked beans, and milk. As they sat down to eat, Pretty turned to Maria with a question hanging in the air.

"Do you have any suggestions on how we can move forward with our lives?" Pretty asked, expecting practical advice.

But instead, Maria's response took a different turn. Tearfully, she opened up about her past, "When I met Michael, I thought I found an angel who would make all my problems disappear. Little did I know, I was fooling myself. Our home was built on deceit. Now, look at me. What have I done to deserve this?"

Trying to comfort her, Pretty said, "Don't cry. The past is gone. We need to focus on the future. You're lucky to be a doctor with your own surgery. I'm worse off — no education, no job."

Maria nodded in understanding but then shared her dilemma, "My surgery brings in some money, but it's not enough. I've tried government hospitals for part-time work, but they have no budget. I need money to pay off credit cards, bills, and maintain the surgery."

Pretty, ever the hustler, suggested a solution, "I'll go back to my hustle job. I know I can make a lot. With the money, I'll attend night school and take a body massage course. Then, I'll set up a Body Massage Parlour."

While Maria supported the idea of a business, she drew a line, "But not a business involving prostitution."

Undeterred, Pretty went back to her hustle. That night, she earned about R4000, paid the owner R1000, and pocketed the rest. Excitedly, she shared the news with Maria, handing her R1500 for being a supportive friend during tough times.

Maria, too, had good news about her day at the surgery, but the money from Medical Schemes would only come at the end of the month. As they sat together, the night unfolded into an unexpectedly enjoyable one.

The next day, Maria had a change of heart about her stance on earning money through prostitution. She decided to team up with Pretty. However, she was worried that her daytime identity as a doctor might be discovered by some clients.

They put their heads together and came up with a plan to move to a less familiar part of the city, away from where they were known. Maria, working as a doctor by day, embraced a different life as a prostitute by night. In just a month, their combined efforts led to more success than they had ever imagined, but it also brought unexpected challenges.

**KOLOBE**

Kolobe, using money from Maria, bought a car and transformed it into a taxi, finding success in his new venture. However, old habits die hard. He returned to his previous criminal ways, engaging in robberies, assaulting people at shebeens, and, whether intentionally or not, causing someone's death. This led to his arrest, conviction, and a death sentence.

During this time, discussions unfolded at CODESA, resulting in the finalization and enactment of the Interim Constitution. In 1995, a landmark decision by the Constitutional Court of South Africa declared that Capital Punishment went against the commitment to human rights outlined in the Interim Constitution. Additionally, section 277(1) (a) of the Criminal Procedure Act of 1977 was invalidated.

Kolobe's life took an unexpected turn as he was spared from hanging by this judgment. Instead, he remained in custody to serve a sentence that would be imposed upon him. The legal changes not only altered Kolobe's fate but also marked a significant step towards upholding human rights in South Africa.

In a hundred sneaky disguises, people betray each other: Through disinterest, emotional neglect, scorn, a shortage of respect, and years of avoiding closeness, as Esther Perel keenly observes.

The Serumula family held a special place in the community's heart. Their kids had it all — education, financial independence — and were the pride of the neighborhood. Yet, within the walls of their seemingly perfect home lurked a different reality, a House of Deceit. The envisioned life for their children remained elusive, respect from the community slipped away, and their once-shining image was tarnished by the shadows of their deceptions.

Sheris astutely pointed out the telltale signs of deceit, shedding light on the hidden fractures within the seemingly idyllic Serumula family.

In a home filled with defensiveness and denial, Ms. Selina Serumula kept a secret that would change everything. She became pregnant within the bounds of marriage but withheld conjugal rights from her husband, as she was secretly involved with the true father of her child.

Facing a lack of intimacy, Mr. Serumula sought solace in a brothel to satisfy his needs, leading to a tragic mistake. His daughter became unintentionally entangled in this web of deceit, falling in love with her half-brother due to her mother's actions.

As the family's secrets unfolded, Kolobe, one of the children, took a dark turn, engaging in robberies, assaults, and eventually committing a heinous crime. The once-close-knit family was unraveling at the seams.

In the aftermath, Peter and Selina divorced, and Peter turned to alcohol, distancing himself from the church. Selina's life took a different path as well; she was dismissed for theft and found herself working as a housekeeper, starting anew in a different role. The house that was once a breeding ground for secrets and turmoil underwent a transformation, each family member finding their own way in the aftermath of a troubled past.

# HISTORY OF MAMELODI

## NOTABLE PEOPLE

**Mayors**:

**First Mayor**. HM Pitjie was the first Mayor. Stadium was named after him: HM Pitjie Statdium.

**Second Mayor**: Mr. A.Kekana: served many years and resigned after his butchery was damaged.

**Third Mayor**: Mr. B.Ndlazi: Played significant role in the service delivery in Mamelodi. However, his success was shadowed by the mass killing of ten people, in 1985.

## Mamelodi Mass Killing of 10 People

The Mamelodi Mass Killing on November 21, 1985, stands as a tragic chapter in history, marking the senseless loss of 10 innocent lives. This horrifying event reflects the devastating impact of violence and the profound need for justice and reconciliation. The memory of those who perished serves as a somber reminder of the collective responsibility to strive for peace, understanding, and a world where such atrocities have no place. May their lives be honored by ongoing efforts to build a more just and compassionate society, fostering unity and healing in the face of past darkness.

On the 21st of November 1985, Mamelodi Residents took to

the streets and marched to the Local Municipality Offices. The aim was to meet the Mayor: Mr B.Ndlazi to address their grievances such as:

**High Rent**

**Banning of week-end Funerals**

Removal of the continued presence of South African Defence Army, Police and the Riots Squad from Mamelodi.

They were told to go to HM Pitjie-not far from those offices.

The Mayor, arrived in an armoured vehicle. Commotion erupted when they told to disperse.

Teargas canisters were thrown at them followed by gunshots.

On the 21st November six people died and the other 4 died the following day

Mr B.Ndlazi was succeeded by Mr. S.S."Drie"Mokone.

During his tenure, he assisted in establishing Moretele Resort Park, extention of Mamelodi for building bounded houses in areas such as Mamelodi Gardens and Moretele View.

**Notable People that made an impact in the Community**

Dr. FF Rubeiro: Medical Doctor, politician and medically assisted many people injured by the Riot Squads.

Ms. Nakedi Ribane: modeller, author and actor above that at the age of 59 years old obtained LLB degree and subsequently admitted as Advocate.

Mr. W.T.Matlala: author. wroted Northern Sotho books.

Mr. M.Ngobeni and Mr A."Tototo" Sibande: ran Karate and Judo schools respectively. Both were Black Belts.

Mr S.Ndhlazi: Body builder.

Mr. M.Phetla and Mr. P.Tefu were some ANC and PAC members imprisoned on Robben Island.

"Skinner Boom" was a group of old timers but not aged. Were used to gather next to a shop of Magodiela. While enjoying their single malt whisky. Engaged in issues of national importance. Some of their members were: The late Human Rights Lawyer: Montsho "Sharks" Sefanyesto, and Bally Mabuse, Desmoo Mabusela, Larrigan Ramasodi and Boy Mafa.

**About The Author**

**Selebogo Stevens Hlongwane** was born and raised in Mamelodi Township, being the sixth child in a family of seven. He is married and blessed with three daughters. Notably, he holds two University Degrees and has earned several post-degree qualifications.

During the 1976 uprising, he actively participated as a shadow activist and played a crucial role in assisting numerous students in securing bursaries for their further education. His commitment extended to initiating employment initiatives in the townships, such as the Car Wash Project, and empowering schoolteachers to assertively engage in courses like Victim to Victor.

In collaboration with the University of South Africa, Selebogo introduced Street Law programs to educate employees on fundamental legal principles. His dedication is evident in his significant contribution to the church, where he actively raised funds for the construction of two large churches.

# Reference

Fortunate Machaba, Tshwane Voice Newspaper & Wilkipedia, embassydirect, sahistory and heart compassion, 2023.

Wikipedia, the free encyclopaedia/ Beer_Hall_Boycott.

Morris E. Goodman; The Miracle Man;1981, Miracle Man Production Inc; 1991.

Kobi Yaamada, What do you do with a problem? July 1, 2016, Compendium.

"George Orwell: Animal Farm, William Collin Publishing, 17 August 1945.

Sheris Stritof: Verywellminded.com/how-to-tell-if-spouse-is-lying-2300996;March 22.2023.

www.ingramcontent.com/pod-product-compliance
Lightning Source LLC
Chambersburg PA
CBHW051436290426
44109CB00016B/1575